Leadership Tidbits
*Powerful Strategies Every Leader
Needs to Know in Order to Win*

Tywauna Wilson, MBA, MLS (ASCP)^{CM}
Visionary Author

Book Cover Design: Little Publishing LLC

Published By: Little Publishing LLC

ISBN: 978-1-7343314-0-0

A Message from the Visionary Author

Greetings, Leadership Trailblazer!

Thank you for embarking on this journey with us. *Leadership Tidbits* is necessary for the success of our workplaces and communities. The purpose of this book is to help movers and shakers shift to the next level in their careers, communities and personal lives.

Early in my career, I identified a gap between current leaders and those who were qualified candidates to confidently transition into leadership positions. Seeing good people get passed over for supervisory roles because they didn't have a strong leadership base troubled me. So, I decided to take action!

When there are not enough qualified candidates to assume these roles, especially when there is an unplanned vacancy, it leads to a breakdown of duties, loss of knowledge, unclear vision and poor morale amongst the team. This leads to inefficiency, miscommunication and chaos, which can be detrimental to an organization! Then, one of two things happen: (1) The organization tries to promote from within, leaving the incumbent having to learn the job and gain leadership skills to be better equipped to thrive in their new role, which can be stressful and overwhelming; or (2) the organization is forced to hire from outside of the organization, which limits the opportunity for internal employees' upward movement. The latter still comes with a learning curve. This is my attempt to bring industry leaders together to provide a practical playbook that one can use to level up on their leadership potential.

As you read through the nuggets of wisdom shared by the mentors in each chapter, take notes, perform your own leadership inventory and create an action plan that you can easily implement in your professional and personal life. If you take the time to do the work, I am confident you will see a positive shift in your life. You have the power to be the change needed, but you must be prepared to act. It will take sacrifice. It will challenge your thinking. But, most importantly, it will require you to bet on *you!*

Grab a pen, set aside some time, open your mind and jump right in! Don't forget to get an accountability partner who will help you stay on track with your goals.

Yours in Leadership,

Tywauna "Coach Tee" Wilson

Dedications

I dedicate my chapter to my daughter, Brooke Brielle, and the next generation of movers and shakers. You have the power to change the world. You can achieve anything that your mind believes is possible. Thank you to my husband Martinez, my mom Helen, and my family and friends for always supporting me on my leadership journey. To my Trendy Elite Leadership Tribe and Trendy Elite Leadership Society bosses, thank you for allowing me to be your fearless leader!

-Tywauna Wilson

I would like to dedicate my chapter to my colleagues in leadership in both education and business. You inspire me every day and I've learned by watching, collaborating, listening, and working alongside you as we all pursue our fanatical goals, dreams, and aspirations. A special shout out to my BGM sisters, your love and support is fanatical. AND to my family and friends, I appreciate you putting up with my fanatical mindset! #fanaticalleadership #leadershipmatters #grateful

-Dr. Christine C. Handy

I dedicate my chapter to aspiring principals of The Next In Line to Lead Aspiring Principal Leadership Academy and aspiring school leaders everywhere. Leadership is not title nor position, but it is about impact and influence. Remember #leadershipmatters

-Dr. Sharon H. Porter

I dedicate this chapter to my daughter, Shardae, and my son, Marcus. They grew up watching me serve as a leader and I know some of my leadership qualities were passed on to them. I see it each day while they are still developing! It amazes me to hear them share about their leadership experiences! May my actions forever impact their journey of serving and making a difference in the lives of other.

-Dr. Essie Mckoy

I dedicate my chapter to every leader searching to find their voice and fighting to find their place in this World. To my husband, mother, family and friends I love you for always telling me the truth and covering my back. To all my Young Kings remember, God First and to the spirit of my Dad and daughter, Niarra I pray I am making you both proud. Grace & Peace

-Alandes Powell

I dedicate my chapter to my children and future leaders - Jarell, Jaden, Jayla, and Jaida. You motivate, inspire and empower me to be a better mom and leader every day. Thank you to my amazing parents - Jeff and Diane Moore and future husband, Derrick Smith for your continued love, encouragement and support on my growth journey. I love you all.

-Jaresha Moore

I would like to dedicate my chapter to my husband, children, family, and every person who has believed in me, encouraged me, supported me and have pushed me to become better.

-Maya Dorsey

Thank you to my children, family, friends, mentors, colleagues and all future leaders reading this, I dedicate this chapter to each of you. Your support, guidance and love provide me with the motivation to keep going and keep growing. You are all very much appreciated. Special thanks to Tywauna Wilson for your vision, leadership and mentorship throughout this book collaboration.

-Tashawna Thomas Otabil

I am grateful for family and dedicate this chapter to the memory of my beloved Mother—Patricia Ocean, my siblings—Beverly, Darrell, and Daniel, and my nieces and nephews. To all my Sistas! Thanks for allowing me to bring my best self to every situation and covering my vulnerabilities. Your support forever sustains me. I pray you are reminded that "you are prepared for the moment you are in".

-Natalie Ocean Canty

I would like to dedicate this collection of leadership tidbits to my parents who have led my family and I in such an incredible way. You have inspired me to go beyond my imagination toward so many dreams that I could never have imagined. Thanks for always modeling love, grace and humility for all those you encounter. The Crystal in me is because of you.

-Dr. Crystal Cooper

I take this precious moment to dedicate this chapter to my husband, Mr. Jeffrey Johnson, and son, Mr. Corey Brunson. I thank you both for encouraging me to write this chapter, so that I may influence future leaders about the importance of adopting a democratic leadership style which can be applied to any organization – schools, businesses, and government. I thank you both for believing in me and loving me always.

-Dr. Melissa A. Brunson

This chapter is dedicated to the memory of my parents Squire and Joyce Williams. You taught me to pursue my purpose and always serve others. I am grateful to my family Carla, Caleb and Asher for always supporting me. You're the reason for my inspiration. I appreciate the many leaders that served as role models for me on my leadership journey. To the next generations of leaders, remember "Up" is a state of mind. Get up and make a difference!

-Dr. Arthur Williams

I dedicate my chapter to my husband who's one of the wisest people I know, to my three beautiful children for their unwavering support — I look forward to watching them grow into leadership using their God given talents. To my Grandmother, Audrey; Mother, Betty; Father, Dennis; Uncle Dwain; and Aunt Kathey. Thank you for your encouragement, family devotion, and most importantly your prayers! I thank God for my family's love. All Glory Belongs to God!

-Lisa Coker

Table of Contents

Dr. Karen Bankston

"Yes, we be the boss! But, we're not bossy. We lead!"

Foreword

I'm a Boss, but I'm Not Bossy!

"I be the boss!" But being the boss is not necessarily the same thing as leading. Leaders bring everyone to the level of their greatest potential. They have the gift of seeing things from a granular level to a broad vision by "connecting the dots." They are able to get their "followers" to see the connections, as well as share in the vision. This system-thinking approach becomes important when leading, as we are now faced with supporting and connecting five generations in the workplace.

Each of these generations (and subgenerations) bring different ways of thinking and behavior to the workplace. Additionally, their expectations surrounding their future, and the role work plays in it, is diverse. Wow! Talk about needing to be skilled at hearing and interpreting several ideologies in order to inspire a shared understanding. This has transformed leadership to an art and a science. Specifically, it becomes important to integrate the psycho-social sciences as a part of our organizational development practices. We must do so "artfully" to ensure that we are encouraging and inspiring well enough to bring forth the best in individuals. Inspiring others, as well as modeling the way, are key factors in leading (Kouzes & Posner, 2015). But how does one do that if they are not motivated as a leader? How do you transform from managing to leading, and from being bossy to being the boss?

"Know what you value and value what you know" is a saying that I coined some 20 years ago as I was in the midst of a large system integration. What I learned is that being cognizant of your personal and professional values is fundamental to your effectiveness to leading others. It supports your willingness to open yourself to other ways of thinking, subsequently allowing yourself to facilitate others to reach their highest potential. Understanding how you feel about concerns that are important to your associates becomes a mandatory assignment when embarking on the journey to leadership. In fact, it should be reflected upon and initiated, prior to the start of the journey.

There is no doubt that you will be faced with challenges as a leader. In order to accept those challenges as opportunities for growth and development, you must endure the process of knowing what is valued (important) to you *prior* to being in the midst of the storm. This whole notion of valuing is grounded in knowing ourselves well enough to establish positive relationships with others so we can share in the responsibility of making effective decisions. And to think, I thought it was just about being the boss!

When I was first privileged to step onto the pathway toward leadership, I had no idea of the importance that building relationships would have on my ability to be successful. In fact, I was completely unaware of the notion of systems and connections in departments, divisions, organizations and beyond. Oh, and by the way, I gained understanding that people retain their hearts and heads when they arrive at work! This revelation came to me when I had critical conversations with individuals who were different than me by age, race, gender and role, to name a few. I had no idea, at the time, the importance of understanding personal, professional and organizational values to get the work done through the people who make up the organization. Nor, as I rose in the ranks of corporate healthcare, did I understand the nuances required for being an African-American female executive in a predominantly white male environment.

I would be remiss if I did not include some thoughts about how being black and female influenced my ability to lead. It is not unknown that, in the United States, we are continually faced with both racial and gender disparities in the workplace. To that end, each of us must call on our own values and practice the art and science of leadership in navigating the environment to be effective. What does that mean? It means that you must: 1) Know and be clear about your values. 2) Reflect on and know who you are as a person and a professional. 3) Be very knowledgeable about the espoused and actual values of the organization. 4) Be willing and able to co-create initiatives that allow for all individuals to be the best that they can be. Navigating the environment using these steps, while adopting an approach based on an intersectionality framework can facilitate all women leaders to success.

Intersectionality, a term coined by Kimberle Williams Crenshaw in 1989, speaks to how different aspects of social identity (race, gender, sexuality and class) contribute to systemic oppression and discrimination. While much of the work done related to intersectionality has focused on issues around the feminist movement, more recent efforts have used this framework to unpack some of the lived experiences of discrimination that black women experience in society. Gaining an understanding of the intersection of race and gender facilitated my reflection of how I fit in the world, both personally and professionally. I was entering into a space that no one in my family had ever gone. So, subsequently, there were no family and no friends to guide or lead me.

At first, there was a sense of isolation and fear of failure. I used this framework and a lot of other references that I could read, as well as my spiritual leader, to "peel the onion" of my life and put it into a new recipe. Through this very active self-development and use of a therapeutic counselor, I achieved a better sense of who I was in these spaces and faced the fear I had personally and professionally. I became a better me!

Becoming a better you, and considering all of the alternatives, is what *Leadership Tidbits* is all about. I am so excited to have been asked to be a part of this collaboration with leaders who have reflected and learned, that, "Yes, we be the boss! But, we're not bossy. We lead!"

References

Crenshaw Williams, K. (1989). *Demarginalizing the Intersection of Race and Sex: A Black Feminist Critique of Antidiscrimination Doctrine, Feminist Theory and Antiracist Politics*. University of Chicago Legal Forum, Vol. 1989, Issue 1.

Kouzes, J.M. & Posner, B. (2012). The Leadership Challenge. 5th Ed. Jossey-Bass

Tywauna Wilson

*I will focus on the areas that will make a positive I.M.P.A.C.T.
in my life and in the lives of others.*

Great Leaders Make an I.M.P.A.C.T.

"Influential people have a profound impact on everyone they encounter. Yet, they achieve this only because they exert so much influence inside, on themselves."

-Travis Bradberry

Are you just starting on your leadership journey? Maybe you have been on the journey for a while but need a refresh. Either way, buckle up! Leadership in today's climate will challenge you to learn, inspire, innovate and connect to be successful. It is a rewarding journey, but know that it is not for the faint of heart. It is tough, but achievable. There are a few key areas I want you to wrap your mind around in order to maximize your leadership role. This will help you move from good to great, from low impact to direct impact, from win to winning.

Every leader should be committed to making an **I.M.P.A.C.T.**:

- ✓ ***Investment*** *in yourself and those around you*
- ✓ ***Mentorship*** *to bring others to the table with you*
- ✓ ***Purpose*** *of why you do what you do*
- ✓ ***Accountability*** *for your goals*
- ✓ ***Collaboration*** *with individuals and organizations so that, collectively, everyone wins*
- ✓ ***Transformation*** *of your thoughts and your actions to move from ordinary to extraordinary*

Good news! These areas are practical and easy enough to implement if you have a desire to do so and are intentional about making a positive I.M.P.A.C.T.!

Investing in Yourself

✓   ***Investment*** *in yourself and those around you*

"Show me a successful person, and I will show you someone who is serious about personal development."

- John Maxwell

"It's not in the budget! If you want to participate in the leadership development program, you will have to pay for the cost of the program yourself." All I could think was, *Wow! I can't believe they are not going to cover the cost. How could they not want to support my professional development? I am one of the best managers on the team… at least that is what was documented in my evaluation. I come to work every day, work long hours, coach and train my team for success, and have made significant strides in making the department more productive than it was the year before.*

Even with all of this, it wasn't enough. I felt like the company was saying that I wasn't worth the investment. Surely, if I was worth the cost, they would find the money to cover the expense, right? It seems like we were always able to find some "hidden" dollars tucked away in budget accounts for other trainings, conferences and celebratory events. So, why couldn't we find it for the leadership development program?

I thought, *They must be crazy! You want me to pay to invest in myself?* Even with all the thoughts running through my head, there was still no money in the budget to cover the $2,500 cost of participating in the leadership development program. I had to make a decision: either pay the cost to participate, or forfeit participating in the program. It was as simple as that. So, the choice was mine. I had to step up and pay up, or not. I don't know why I was going back and forth. It wasn't about the money. I had the money to pay for the program, but I had to convince myself that I was *worth* the cost. I had to believe that I was worth the investment. This was the first mindset shift that I had about investing in my professional development. How could I be mad at my employer for not investing in me if I was unwilling to invest in myself?

How many times on your leadership journey have you had to make the decision to personally invest in yourself? As leaders, in order to be able to grow our teams, we must be able to grow ourselves. It is hard to spark innovation if we become comfortable and stagnant in our own growth. Outside of a formal education or certification, most people will not commit to being intentional about ongoing personal and professional development. There is this notion that the degree or education that one has already will sustain them throughout their career. This is far from the truth. Today's ceiling is the floor for tomorrow. To be the best, and sit at the table with the best, we must continue to grow and develop daily. Those who are at the table are investing, which is why they remain at the table.

Opportunities for Investing in Your Growth:

Attend a Conference in Your Niche: Staying in the loop of advances in your field of expertise will allow you to have a relevant perspective.

Join a Masterclass: Learn from an expert who is teaching a focus topic in your industry.

Hire a Coach: Coaches help guide you to reach an agreed-upon goal, typically over a specified period. This is more like a partnership. Coaches help you change your behavior without injecting their own personal experience. They help you find the solutions within yourself.

Listen to Podcasts: A great way to get insight from industry professionals is on the go. Popular podcasts can be found on iTunes, Podbean, Sound Cloud and other outlets. Some of these are free, while others require a fee.

Subscribe to Being a Lifelong Learner: Remember, leaders are readers! They are not just readers of books, but of people and situations. I recommend two practical books for your bookshelf, both by John Maxwell: *The 15 Invaluable Laws of Growth* and *Developing the Leader Within You 2.0*. These focus on personal growth and leadership. *Think and Grow Rich* by Napoleon Hill is a great book on transforming your mindset. All of these can be found as audiobooks, as well.

From Mentee to Mentor

> ✓ ***Mentorship*** *to bring others to the table with you*

The relationship between a mentor and mentee consists of empowerment by the leader. This includes influencing others with the purpose of investing into their lives so that they can reach their highest personal and professional growth. It is a gift for both the mentee and the mentor.

When I think about full circle mentorship, I think about my relationship with one of my favorite mentees, Monia. We met in 2012 when she was a freshman at the University of Cincinnati. She came over to my office to bring some flyers about the university's Medical Laboratory Science Program. She was supposed to get a tour of the laboratory, as well. But, when she got there, she was improperly dressed and not prepared for the tour. As I was walking her out, I thanked her for bringing the flyers. I also told her that she could benefit from going through the college's mentoring program. I was a mentor in the program, but I already had a mentee.

I said, "They'll connect you with a mentor in the field of medical laboratory science, and I think you would benefit greatly from that."

Instead, she went to the program director and asked to be paired with me. We were then connected and have been connected ever since. I helped her with interviewing and strategically selecting her clinical training site. I shared expertise with her to set the foundation for a solid experience of being a medical laboratory scientist. When I would meet with Monia, it was clear that, since I was opening doors and pouring into her, when she graduated from school and had a few years' experience in the profession, she would return to the program and serve as a mentor for someone else. She made good on that promise when she graduated. She became the mentor to a young scientist named Taz. Her expectation of Taz was the same that I had for her a few years prior. This is how true mentorship should work. Great mentors will use their influence to provide access and opportunity. They will become champions for their mentees. They help their mentees get into rooms that they may not be able to get into otherwise.

You Have to Know Where You Are In Order to Know Where You Are Going

✓ ***Purpose*** *of why you do what you do*

As you continue on your leadership journey, there will be times when you are running ninety miles per hour and you lose focus on the "why" behind it. There will be challenges, changes, twists and turns that may cause you to lose the passion behind your why. It's in these times when you need constant reminders that you are on the right track.

I had to remind myself of this when I was in the early stages of building a mobile healthcare outreach program from the ground up. This uniquely integrated program incorporated screening mammography and point-of-care laboratory testing. The van serviced women where they worked and where they lived, with the goal of providing access to healthcare for all women. Our goal was to reduce the number of unknown breast cancer diagnoses. However, this initiative was met with many barriers, including securing grants for those who had no insurance, struggling to find staff who was properly licensed to drive the 40-foot van, language barriers, technology limitations in rural areas, as well as weather limitations.

It seemed like the more we tried to get our van on the road, the more challenges we came up against. There were days when we would arrive onsite to perform our healthcare screenings, only to find that we had an issue with our equipment, which caused us to reschedule patients. Other times, we had a schedule full of patients, but very few actually showed up. During the first year of operation, we were met with challenge after challenge; yet, we kept pushing. The patience of the team grew weary. Finally, there was a breakthrough and it all began to click. We found ways to streamline our processes so that equipment breakdowns became less of a challenge. The program gained more exposure. We started seeing more patients and the program became the signature outreach program in the area. Thank goodness we didn't give up. Thank goodness we remained committed to our purpose.

There will be times when the barriers you come up against become distractions for your why. This happens in our workplace all the time, but it also happens within ourselves as leaders. If you are unclear of your purpose, and you don't know your why, a deep-dive self-discovery is needed to gain clarity. It is important to know where you stand long before you make decisions that may compromise your core values. When you are clear on your strengths, your core values and your purpose, regardless of how busy you get, or how unclear the road ahead may be, you will not lose focus on the reason you started on the journey in the first place. This allows you to remain steadfast in pressing toward the goal.

Action Speaks Louder Than Words

✓ ***Accountability for*** *your goals*

Most successful leaders have a personal board of directors, who help them stay accountable to their goals. Your board of directors will be honest with you and tell you the truth, no matter how difficult it may be to hear. They also provide the gift of feedback. It is easy to come up with goals and action plans for your life. But if there is no one to keep you accountable, you may never see the goals come to fruition.

I recently participated in an accountability partnership program. I talked about being overwhelmed with trying to complete all of the tasks on my project list. My board member had recently completed a similar program and was pleased with the outcome. The program was six weeks, but focused on completing only one to two goals during that time. My partners and I met every week for 30 minutes to discuss our progress during that week and our action for the next week. At the end of the program, I completed both of my goals. These were goals that I had put off for months. It was something about having others cheer me to the finish line, but not allowing me to give up or procrastinate, that pushed me even harder. The strategic ideas from my partners and the weekly check-ins were instrumental in moving me forward to the next level. It was fulfilling to be able to achieve what I set forth in such a short amount of time. If you are struggling with keeping yourself accountable, get you an accountability team!

Together We Are Better

✓ ***Collaboration*** *with individuals and organizations so that, collectively, everyone wins*

"Collaboration is not about gluing together existing egos. It's about the ideas that never existed until after everyone entered the room."

~ Kathleen McNeeny

Leaders are not afraid to work with other leaders to achieve a common goal. Several years ago, I went to Rwanda, Africa as a global consultant for the American Society for Clinical Pathology (ASCP) as part of an initiative to combat HIV/AIDS in their country. ASCP was looking for U.S. industry experts to collaborate with the laboratorians in Africa. I was fortunate to be selected to teach them clinical chemistry and lab safety so that they were able to be better lab scientists. After the training, they were able to go back to their respective labs across the country and train their teams on the new techniques they learned. As lab scientists, we were able to come together and learn from each other in order to have a widespread impact. While I was there training them, I learned so much about myself and gained better training techniques.

When we collaborate with other individuals, teams and organizations, we multiply our efforts. In leadership, you don't have to know everything all the time. There is strength in our connections. Through our collaborative efforts, we can have a larger, more diverse reach.

From Ordinary to Extraordinary

✓ ***Transformation*** *of your thoughts and your actions to move from ordinary to extraordinary*

In order to experience transformational change, it will require you to be persistent and dedicated. It doesn't matter if it hasn't been done before or it seems impossible. I will continue to knock down doors. Sometimes, the people at the table don't know that they need you at the table until after you have arrived and offered your fresh perspective.

When you come to an environment, don't be afraid to bring transformational ideas to the table. Nothing moves forward if everyone thinks on the same level.

The same is true in our personal life. We have to challenge and stretch our thinking to get out-of-the-box results. We have to get comfortable being uncomfortable. This could mean participating in an activity that is foreign to you so that you have a better understanding of others' viewpoints. There is a lesson in every assignment, but you have to be open to receive it. Ordinary thinking will never result in extraordinary results!

Great leaders make an I.M.P.A.C.T.! First, you must start with making a difference in your own life. Second, commit to making an impact in the lives of those around you. Finally, train up others to make an impact so that the efforts are multiplied. Being an impactful leader shouldn't rest solely on your shoulders, but on the collective efforts of us all!

1. In what areas of your leadership do you need to invest more?

2. Do you have a personal board of directors? If so, who are they and what role do they serve in your life?

3. What is your "why" statement?

Tashawna Thomas Otabil

*I will engage in positive, productive and supportive
mentoring relationships that help me thrive.*

The Importance of Mentorship

"Show me a successful individual and I'll show you someone who had real positive influences in his or her life. I don't care what you do for a living—if you do it well, I'm sure there was someone cheering you on or showing you the way. A mentor."

— Denzel Washington

The definition of mentorship is the guidance provided by a mentor, especially an experienced person in a company or educational institution. Mentorships are a significant part of your overall personal and professional success. A good, strong mentor will provide support, guidance and emotional support to help stimulate personal growth. As business professionals, it is important to have support with communication, decision-making, networking and goals. Mentorship is an excellent resource to help navigate through possible challenges that are thrown our way, such as getting passed over for promotions, problems with a co-worker, improving business acumen or time management.

Mentors are also typically well-connected. This will open a lot of networking opportunities for development since mentors usually introduce their mentees to others with the purposeful intent to assist them with achieving their goals. Mentors are inspiring. They help motivate and build confidence. Mentors want to see their mentees succeed.

Mentors are authentic and objective. If you need to change your attitude, or you need to change how you deal with situations, they will tell you. Feedback enriches the process for the exchange of ideas and opinions. It will help you become more self-aware and grounded. Mentors can be career coaches or career champions for your personal or professional success.

Goals of Mentoring

"Choose your mentors based on who you want to be. Mentors can reflect where you want to go; they can create access for you and give you guidance as you plan your own personal development."

— Ranu Gupta

You will not recognize the value of mentorship until you have a mentor. One of the first steps in creating a successful mentoring relationship is for both the mentor and mentee to identify, define and establish goals.

A mentoring relationship should be defined from the beginning. Determine how often you will connect. Will you meet on a weekly, monthly or quarterly basis? How long will the meeting be? Will this be a short-term or long-term relationship? What are your desired outcomes? Both parties have to be committed to the relationship by choice. Each should openly share his or her goals for the relationship and work collaboratively to achieve them.

No matter the course, foundationally, it's important for you to trust and respect your mentor. Your mentor will provide you with expert guidance, feedback and support based on his or her personal and business experiences. They openly share opinions and ideas based on the challenges they have lived through. The key to getting the most out of the relationship is determined by your ability to enter into the relationship with an open mind. Avoid being judgmental and be coachable.

You also need to be authentic. Your mentor needs to know the *real you*. Share your values, strengths, challenges, goals and aspirations. If you are not willing to be transparent, your mentor will not be able to provide you with the appropriate context to offer counsel and the support you need.

As the mentee, you also need to decide what you need. Are you seeking career advancement? Are you trying to enhance your professional network? Are you looking to improve your professional or business acumen? Do you need help with improving your communication skills? Perhaps you're looking for encouragement to help you continue moving forward. Deciding what you need will be essential in helping you align with the appropriate mentor.

Lastly, be flexible. While in-person meetings bring an atmosphere of making a better connection, be open to teleconference and virtual communications, as well. Not everyone has the time to physically connect, but they can still be a great mentor. I have several mentors. One of my favorite mentors lives in another state. We've known each other over seventeen years. She's smart, strategic and extremely knowledgeable. The level of experience and insight she has as a C-Suite executive in corporate America, as well as an entrepreneur, has been invaluable. We've arranged to meet virtually (FaceTime, Skype) once every other month.

Having virtual connections allows us to have the personal connection, and it provides an opportunity to do a true "pulse check" on how respective I am to feedback. She observes my nonverbal communications and facial expressions to understand my state of mind. She assesses my engagement, or lack thereof, and is able to see whether I'm excited, frustrated, sad or uncomfortable with the topic. Being able to make these observations helps her understand my level of emotional intelligence, as well as the places where she needs to continually challenge me. The positive impact of her words and her accountability has been a critical component of my growth and success.

Finding the Right Blend

"A mentor is someone who allows you to see the hope inside yourself. A mentor is someone who allows you to know that, no matter how dark the night, in the morning, joy will come. A mentor is someone who allows you to see the higher part of yourself when sometimes it becomes hidden to your own view."

– Oprah Winfrey

Mentor selections can vary based on personal and professional needs. It's important to note that finding someone in the same industry, ethnic background and/or gender should not be a qualitative factor. Consider opening yourself up to a wide range of perspectives and different opportunities to learn.

A good mentor will learn your personal strengths and weaknesses. Find a mentor who will help you focus on your weaknesses, so they can complement your strengths. Mentors should break you out of your comfort zone. They should encourage you to be comfortable with being uncomfortable, so you can keep improving and walk into new experiences. Expect the unexpected!

Recognize perception versus reality. Your vision may differ from the reality of things. It is important that you trust your mentor enough to be honest and transparent. Ask those hard questions that you may not be comfortable with addressing with your leader or in another professional setting. When you encounter a difficult issue at work, and need some input or guidance, your mentor is your primary source. Recently, I discussed an issue with one of my internal mentors (individual who works within the organization) on how to best manage my leader's perception about me looking for other job opportunities. Because I am an extrovert, I make new connections, experience different things and, most importantly, I constantly strive to improve myself daily.

Learning the culture and environment of the organization I am working for is important to me. I take it upon myself to meet with various department leaders and executives, so I can fully understand why they do what they do and how I might be able to learn or contribute. As I was making my rounds through the organization, I often got feedback from my leader, indicating that she was aware of me meeting with the other leaders. She constantly asked why I was looking to get out of my current position. Again, this was her perception. I reiterated to her that I was looking for opportunities to expand my knowledge and grow. It wasn't about "getting out." No matter what response I gave, I still couldn't seem to manage her perception. It made me uncomfortable and caused anxiety.

I addressed the situation with my mentor, expecting him to side with me. In fact, his response was the opposite. The first question he asked was, "Where is your succession plan?"

I said, "I don't have one."

"Well, you are your own problem," he said.

He went on to express how large my role was and how difficult it would be to find a replacement. Having a succession plan would reduce anxiety for me and assist with managing my leader's perception. She wouldn't be concerned about the position of the department once someone else filled that position. I was so appreciative of his feedback. He helped me to pause and ultimately reflect to consider a different point of view that helped me solve the issue. This was a tremendous gift.

Mentor "Beware"

I'm sure you have heard the phrase that "everything that appears to be good is not got for you." The same statement is true as it relates to mentors. All mentors are not good and therefore, they may not be good for you. There is a difference between a bad mentor and one who is wrong for *you*. For example, receiving advice from someone who hasn't been through similar experiences might not be beneficial. On the same note, having a mentor who is constantly saying negative, discouraging things to you about their boss and/or company, is probably not a good mentor. It's important to beware of certain characteristics and behaviors that can be detrimental to your growth.

Another characteristic of a bad mentor is one who believes that they have no room to improve. There is always room for continuing education and improvement. Good mentors continue to educate you as well as themselves. They are consistently talking on additional trainings, attending seminars/webinars and seeking network opportunities. If you have a mentor who is constantly discussing how they perform better than their peers or leaders or how they hold all the information or should be leading in a role instead of someone else, *beware*—the know-it-all, doesn't know it all! Mentors lead and teach by example. These examples are not of one you should follow.

Some mentor relationships start off well, where the mentor can appear to be very attentive and offer support and advice. But then they fall off. There is no follow through on the promises made, seems to be a lack of engagement on issues that are important to you and they continue to be "too busy" or reschedule meetings. This doesn't necessarily mean that this person is a bad mentor. They just may not have time for you at that time. Perhaps they were over committed with the agreement to be your mentor. This is very common. My recommendation would be to discontinue the mentorship and seek out a replacement. Specifying a mentoring plan upfront and create an accountability plan with your mentor will help you achieve the best results.

Underuse & Overuse of Mentorships

Mentors are free. Do you know how valuable it is to have a free resource who provides a wealth of knowledge and experiences? A person who speaks life into you, provides a listening ear, as well as support and guidance? They are, in fact, priceless and they should not be taken for granted.

Key things to consider to get the most out of your mentorship:

- Take the initiative to seek a mentor. You are in control of your growth and development.
- Respect their time. Honor the commitment and meeting arrangements you agreed upon.
- Act on their advice. They can see where you need to improve. Listen.
- Use the tools and resources they provide you. You should not expect your mentor to solve all your problems. Take advantage of their networks and resources. Do not shy away from opportunities.
- You should not allow your personal relationship to influence your decisions or discussion. You are likely to become close with the person who is mentoring you, but don't allow this to take precedence over your overall goals.

- Ask for feedback. Accept criticism. Accept that you will make mistakes.
- Remove your ego. Everyone has something to learn.
- Say, "Thank you!" Express your gratitude and appreciation for your growth and development.

No matter where you are in your career, mentors can energize you and help enhance your personal development, as well as accelerate your career path. Having a mentor is a sign of strength. It demonstrates that you are smart enough and are driven enough to succeed. Be encouraged. Be inspired. Commit to the process. Be great!

As you think about your mentorship journey, I challenge you with the following questions.

- Will you take the initiative to find a mentor or mentors?

- How will you ensure that the mentor you select is the right blend?

- Leaders lead. Are you willing to pay this forward and become a mentor to others?

Dr. Christine C. Handy
*I am committed to helping others bring out the
crazy winner inside and realize their crazy goals,
dreams and aspirations. I am a Fanatical Leader!*

Six Keys to Fanatical Leadership

"Passion is everything. In fact, you've got to be borderline fanatical about what you do!"
-Chris Gardner

I was a leader before I was a teenager. The oldest in a family of five children with a single mother, I was forced to lead my siblings to help my mother. I was responsible for cooking, helping with homework, supervising chores and babysitting. My siblings would describe me as "doing the most." As I look back, I call that "leadership!"

I loved being in charge. I loved being the one who Mom depended on to "get the job done." I loved being the one my siblings could count on. They looked up to me, and I could not let them down. I had to take care of them. I had to be responsible for them and keep them safe. I had to support them and, most importantly, love them. As crazy as that might have been for a young kid, I took great pride in this responsibility. I did it with a degree of excellence and, as a result, my single mother was relieved and delighted that she could depend on me.

Eventually, I passed these leadership skills on to the neighborhood. One summer, I wrote a curriculum to teach a cooking class to the local children and presented it to a director at the local recreation center. They were impressed and accepted my proposal. I was 13 years old at the time. As a result, I taught cooking skills to 15 children and all of the cooking supplies were paid for by the recreation center.

I was also a Girl Scout. While Mom really did not have the money to fund all my crazy whims and desires to be in organizations with other like-minded girls, she always "rubbed two nickels together," as she would say, and made it happen. In the Girl Scouts, I always pledged to help people and to make the world a better place. In the Girl Scouts, I learned to set goals (to earn badges); to plan (what actions I would take to earn those badges); to celebrate accomplishments with others; and to give back to the community. I learned that personal growth was important and that developing leadership skills would pay off eventually.

Thank you, Girl Scouts of America.

As life would have it, I have been a leader for as long as I can remember. Throughout high school and college, I led student organizations and events. In my career, I have served as a teacher leader, head coach, and a high school principal for over 20 years. I went on to be the first woman of color to lead one of the largest professional education organizations in the nation, serving as president of the National Association of Secondary School Principals (NASSP). Through NASSP, I refined my leadership skills and developed new ones. I was prepared to serve as a voice for school leaders, to lead the nation's secondary principals' organization, and to serve as the chair of the board of directors. Trust me, that was crazy rewarding!

When I reflect on my past, and consider my future as a leader, the word "fanatical" comes to mind. Fanatical is defined as "insane with enthusiasm," "filled with excessive and single-minded zeal," and "excessively devoted." Leadership is crazy. To be a great leader, you must be fanatical! Think about Jeff Bezos, the CEO and founder of Amazon. He's a visionary and master builder. He had a crazy idea to change how we shop, and he has truly changed the world with his concept of online shopping. Although he is known for having high expectations and for being a demanding leader, thousands aspire to work for him.

Geoffrey Canada, the CEO of the Harlem Children's Zone, had a vision that all children could excel academically, regardless of their zip code and circumstances, through recalibrating expectations and providing wrap-around services in schools to include medical, social and education support, starting at birth. Today, he has served more than 12,000 children and 95% of them have gone on to college from a neighborhood in Harlem, New York. His unusual outcomes have caused people to model his program across the nation.

Howard Schultz, the CEO of Starbucks, turned a small Seattle coffee retail business into a coffee experience that is now worldwide, with more than 29,000 locations. He had this crazy idea to give part-time employees benefits, such as medical insurance, paid leave and scholarships for higher education. Barack Obama, a leader devoted to community activism, had the crazy notion to make a bigger impact in the world by running for President of the United States of America. He won and became the 44th President, the first African-American president in the USA.

Fanatical leaders are like electricity. They bring the energy that propels a team forward, from good to great, taking it to the next level. To be an amazing leader who truly makes a difference in any area, you must be fanatical. You must be *crazy*, which means passionate or extremely excited. You are the plug. You bring the electricity and the power! There are six keys to fanatical leadership:

- Crazy Purpose
- Crazy Mindset
- Crazy Game Plan
- Crazy Learning
- Crazy Resilience
- Crazy Mentorship

Crazy Purpose

What sets your soul on fire? What makes you jump out of bed, eager to start your day? Why do you do *it*? What is the impact that you want to make in your space? These are questions that you must be able to answer to be a fanatical leader. A fanatical leader has a *big why*! Your crazy purpose is what motivates you to do *it*. I don't know what your *it* is, but you sure as heck need to know what *it* is and why you do *it*.

I am a high school principal and an entrepreneur, and I am always on the go. What keeps me going is my crazy purpose. I am determined to develop winners and to help others realize their goals, dreams and aspirations. During the day, that is my amazing students, the administrative team and the staff. After school, it is the incredible people on my team of wellness entrepreneurs who have big dreams of financial independence. When your *why* is *big*, it gives you energy. It propels you and it drives you. I always tell people that I work from *can* to *can't*. From the time I wake up in the morning, to the time when I can't hold my eyes open, I work.

Take the time to identify your crazy purpose. Spend some time journaling and writing a personal purpose statement. Writing a personal purpose statement will help you align your core ambitions with your actions. It connects to what you want to accomplish, why it is important to you, and how you will realize your goals, dreams and aspirations as a fanatical leader. Dream big and take the limits off! This is a key to success.

Crazy Mindset

Have you lost your mind? You better! To be a fanatical leader, you must lose your mind. In my presentations, I tell attendees, "When you lose your mind, you change your life for the better." Fanatical leaders do not think like "normal" leaders. They have a *crazy mindset*. They are optimistic, always seeing the glass as half full, never half empty. They are positive and see the bright side of negativity. They experience growth from trials. They fail forward. They have crazy faith, and they believe in themselves and their team. They believe in their purpose and are driven to be successful. They set big goals and they are relentless in pursuit of them. They surround themselves with like-minded, success-oriented people. They have a crazy work ethic and are willing to do what it takes to achieve their goals. They write "I am" statements and post them where they can see them every day. A crazy mindset is energizing and will propel you to the next level. You can't always control what is happening around you, but you do control how you think about it and how you respond. So, I ask you again, "Have you lost your mind?" It is a key process on your leadership journey.

Crazy Game Plan

A fanatical leader always has a game plan. They say, "Failure to plan is planning to fail." Do you think Tony Dungy, the first African-

American NFL coach to win the Super Bowl, showed up to a game without a game plan? Of course not. In order to win the game, you must have a strategy, a prepared team and a good mix of core of leaders. You must be ready. I like to ask my high school athletes on game day if they are ready for the game in the evening.

They usually respond, "Yeah, we're ready!"

I tell them that, "In the future, you should say, 'We stay ready!' If you stay ready, you don't have to get ready."

A fanatical leader stays ready. They are like a GPS. They know where they are going, how they will get there and when they need to reroute. Fanatical leaders are intentional. They use data and information to analyze their position. They are visionary leaders; thus, they focus on where they want to take their team, business or organization. With my wellness team, I like to have individualized strategy sessions. This helps me to learn about their goals, to help them dream big, and to help him or her set a crazy game plan. I love big dreamers because they know that it won't be easy, but they are willing to work for it. Planning is an essential key to success for fanatical leadership. It is like fuel for the plane. You can't take off without a plan.

Crazy Learner

Fanatical leaders are crazy about learning, about their own personal growth and the growth of their team. Leaders are readers. In this era of audiobooks, they may be listeners, too. Either way, they are about getting better each day. They are about growth! Crazy learners read. They listen to podcasts. They attend conferences and conventions. They network, blog and take online courses. They participate in professional learning communities. They desire to learn more and are overly committed to their own personal and professional development. They are driven to be the best and believe that learning is key to their development.

In order to "bloom where you are planted," you must be fertilized and watered to grow. I am a book nerd. I have more books on leadership and personal development than my home library can hold. My Kindle library is overflowing, too. I want to take in as much information as I can to help me be the best leader that I can be. An imperative key to success is crazy learning. Be a student of your sport. Be coachable and stay ready!

Crazy Resilience

A rubber band, when stretched, is designed to spring right back into shape. They are made from rubber, which has superior elasticity that helps it to be flexible and to bounce right back. A fanatical leader is just like that rubber band. When you are stretched or tested, or when you experience adversity or trials, you must have the capacity to recover quickly and bounce back. You must have crazy resilience. As a leader, you will experience trials and tribulations. However, a religious leader once said, "Fear not." A fanatical leader is strong and resilient. They can withstand the tests and trials. People will bring negativity into your space. Things will not always go as you planned. You may not reach the goals that you set. Your team may not be on one accord, but you cannot break. As the leader, you show others the way. You are the example, the rubber band and the glue that holds it all together. Snap back!

Crazy resilience includes failing forward. John Maxwell says, "Sometimes we win. Sometimes we learn." Resilience is looking at failure as a learning opportunity. Sometimes when you are innovative, or when you take risks, it doesn't work out. But, I promise you, that if you analyze *why* it didn't work, what would have made it better, and what would be a better way to pursue it next time, the outcome will be much better than the risk. Willie Jolley said it best: "A setback is just a set up for a comeback!" Crazy resilience is a key for fanatical leadership.

Crazy Mentorship

Mentoring plays a crucial role in cultivating future leaders. Oprah Winfrey, a media executive and billionaire philanthropist, defines a mentor in this way: "A mentor is someone who allows you to see the hope inside yourself." Fanatical leaders do not keep all their knowledge and expertise to themselves. They desire to support others by mentoring them and taking great pride in their success. My personal purpose statement includes helping others to develop the winner within. I take great pride in helping others realize their goals, dreams and aspirations.

A mentor develops positive relationships and helps their mentees focus on career and personal growth goals. I am proud that nine of my assistant principals have gone on to become principals, four custodians have become building managers, numerous teachers have become department chairs, and former students have gone to college and graduated. In business, I mentor wealth warriors who are striving for financial freedom. Zig Ziglar says, "You can have everything in life that you want if you help others get what they want." That's mentoring.

I also have personal mentors of my own. It is not enough to just *be* a mentor. Fanatical leaders need mentors, too. Find someone who is doing what you want to do and ask them to serve as your mentor. As a teacher leader, I asked a principal if she would be my mentor. I paid attention to how she navigated her school community and the challenges that she faced. We met regularly and she pushed my thinking. Her mentoring helped mold me into the school leader that I am today. In business, I have several millionaire mentors. They have accomplished what I dream to accomplish. I am paying attention! Mentoring is a key to your success as a fanatical leader. Fanatical leaders are needed to drive organizations, businesses and teams to their highest potential.

Call to Action

A. What is your crazy purpose? Write your personal purpose statement.

B. "I am" statements are powerful affirmations. What you write after, "I am" will come to be if you believe and are willing to work for it. Write three, "I am" statements and read them to yourself daily.

1.

2.

3.

C. Identify three people who you will mentor this year.

1.

2.

3.

D. What steps are you taking toward crazy learning?

E. When you are challenged, what steps will you take to be crazy resilient?

Recommended Reading

- *Uncommon: Finding Your Path to Significance* by Tony Dungy

- *The 21 Irrefutable Laws of Leadership: Follow Them and People Will Follow You*
  by John C. Maxwell

- *Leadershift: The 11 Essential Changes Every Leader Must Embrace* by John C. Maxwell

- *The Anomaly Mind-Set: How I Transformed My Business and My Life by Standing Out Instead of Fitting In* by Sandi Krakowski

- *Dare to Lead* by Brené Brown

- *The Power of Positive Leadership* by Jon Gordon

- *Start with Why: How Great Leaders Inspire Everyone to Take Action* by Simon Sinek

Dr. Sharon H. Porter

*"Passion, Persistence and Perseverance
is the hallmark of effective leadership."*

Leadership Matters

I earned my fifth degree in educational leadership in 2017 from Howard University. This was after *not* being able to complete a prior doctoral program between 2006 and 2012. I eventually removed myself from the first program and chose to earn an educational specialist degree with the credits I'd already earned. Two years after *settling* for a specialist degree, I started over.

In the summer of 2014, I enrolled in Howard University's EAGLE III program. I was determined to finish what I had started. Not only was I completing my coursework for the doctoral program, writing my dissertation and working full-time in a large urban school district, but I decided to write my first book and start my coaching and consulting business simultaneously. All in the name of leadership. Somewhere in between all of those tasks, I started a third podcast entitled *Leadership Matters*.

Over the last three years, I have been interviewing educational leaders from across the world. What I have now discovered after being a part of the entrepreneurial space is that leadership is leadership, no matter the industry. In my quest to understand the journeys of these leaders, I also aimed to discover some of the best practices implemented in schools and school districts across the globe. Again, many of the best practices in the business industry turned out to be solid practices in education.

I ask specific questions that relate to the work of each leader, but they each are asked the same last question, "Why, in your opinion, does leadership matter?" I have chosen to share some of the most insightful responses that can certainly be transferred to a variety of leadership entities.

"The very essence of leadership is that you have to have vision.
You can't blow an uncertain trumpet.

~ Theodore M Hesburgh

Vision, by far, was the response most discussed as it relates to leadership. It has been said that vision is the secret to leadership success. Every great accomplishment has effective leadership with vision behind it. Leadership matters because its capabilities directly impact an organization. A leader must have vision. There is no leadership without vision.

"You don't have to hold a position in order to be a leader."

– Henry Ford

Leadership matters simply because it is not about position or title. You lead where you are. It was my first year teaching in Charlotte, North Carolina. I had just graduated in December 1991 from Winston-Salem State University, earning a bachelor's degree in elementary education. Although I had completed a semester of student teaching, I still felt like I was moving toward the unknown. Somehow, the thought of being responsible for educating the minds of these fourth graders scared me. Could I do it? Would they actually learn? I decided at that point that I would take command of my class to ensure that the students received what they needed to succeed. I wasn't necessarily thinking about leadership when I made this conscious decision. But, as I look back on those early years of my educational career, I know this was the beginning of me leading.

"The art of leadership is saying no, not yes. It is very easy to say yes."

~Tony Blair

Leadership matters because when it's time to have the courageous conversations, the effective leader can handle the discomfort that comes with those difficult conversations. It certainly is simpler to respond in favor of someone's request. It matters when you can make decisions based on the evidence or what's best for the organization as a whole, not individuals.

"Lead from the back and let others believe they are in front."
~Nelson Mandela

Leadership matters because as leaders, you must know the work cannot be accomplished alone. I learned that you can get more accomplished as the *guide on the side* versus the *sage on the stage* when you are leading. I saw an increase in my business, as well as in the productivity within my organization, when I demonstrated shared leadership. Why is it that some people have greater influence than others? It's because of the relationships that have been established. When you allow shared or distributed leadership, you build trust. When you build trust, you are strengthening relationships. When you lead from the back, you are in fact leading from the front.

"What you do has far greater impact than what you say."
~ Stephen Covey

Action speaks louder than words. Leadership matters because, as a leader, actions are key to success. I am an early riser. I am intentional and deliberate. My best work is finalized in the darkness of the morning. The deliberate act of waking up at 3 a.m. every morning has benefitted me in more ways than imaginable.

I first discovered my "magical" hour while completing my undergraduate study. While other classmates I knew would pull all-nighters when studying, I would be fast asleep. I would awaken, refreshed and ready to put in the work hours before class. It worked for me then, and it continues to work for me now.

During my second round in the doctoral program, my dissertation advisor and I met every Saturday to review my research. She offered feedback and suggestions. One particular week, I had made plans to do something else that weekend and I wasn't going to meet for the dissertation session. I sent my advisor an email, informing her that I would not be meeting for the session. I was taken aback when her response was simply, "Ok." At that moment, I realized that I had to take accountability for my own progress. My dissertation advisor was already minted with a terminal degree. Here I was, in a second doctoral program, after not completing the first program, and I had the nerve to email her to say, "I won't be attending." I took her simple, yet profound response as, "It's on you." Needless to say, I did not miss a session after that one.

Leadership matters because effective leaders take ownership of their success and the success of the organization. The ability to learn is the most important quality a leader can possess. Learner is one of my top five strengths for the CliftonStrengths assessment. The process of learning is what is most intriguing to me. It has never been about the number of degrees earned; it is simply about the knowledge gained. An effective leader knows that they do not have all of the answers. They continually seek more meaning, growth and development. Being a lifelong learner is inevitable.

Leadership is influence. Leaders focus on behaviors that produce results. As a leader, you must act, assess and adjust. We must be able to impact behaviors, attitudes and opinions.

Leading with vision, compassion and transparency are my core values. I take pride in building relationships and understanding that just because you can do something, doesn't mean you should. In leadership, trust, as well as establishing and maintaining positive relationships, matters. People do business with people they know, like and trust. As a leader, we are charged with the responsibility of allowing individuals to feel they are safe to make mistakes and take risks. The growth of the organization depends upon it.

Leadership matters in education, in corporate America, in entrepreneurship, in sports and in every other facet of life. Your leadership effectiveness is measured by the success of those who follow you. As a leader, my main focus is to develop and inspire others to greatness.

As I begin my tenth year in school leadership (in title), but my thirtieth year as an influencer, my passion continues to remain with novice leaders. Whether it is skill or will that I am nurturing in first-time school leaders, I remain steadfast in encouraging them to lead from the heart. Leadership Matters!

Questions

1. Who has had a positive impact on you as a leader?

2. What are specific leadership behaviors that have yielded positive results in your career, business or life?

3. Commitment is demonstrated through action. In what ways do you follow through on your commitments?

Dr. Essie McKoy

*Leadership is an action that allows me to serve
others while elevating my capacity! My impact and ability
to make systemic changes will be a part of my legacy!*

Traits of An Effective Leader

According to Vinci Lombardi, "Leaders are made, they are not born!" Most of us have heard that saying, but when you really think about being an effective, impactful leader, I invite you to embrace the idea that you will need to be crafted. That has been my experience as I have travelled the leadership path!

In this chapter, I will not only get you to analyze your own leadership journey, the type of leader you are presently, and what makes you a great leader, but I will discuss traits of effective leaders. Also, I will share leadership lessons and leadership nuggets that I have learned in my 30+ years of serving and making a difference. Interestingly, I share while I am still on that journey of leading and making an impact.

While it felt as though I was born to be a leader, I took the leadership journey that had unforeseen destinations. I encountered some challenging situations and learned some tough lessons along the way. Those challenges and lessons are what made me into the leader I am today! I believe that if you do not stretch your abilities, heighten your awareness of effective leadership strategies, or search within your leadership core, you will not reach the pinnacle of great leadership!

There are days that will seem like you have been to the mountaintop in your role as a leader. Then, there are days in which you will feel like you have gone to the lowest valley. The most important aspect is to always remember that those feelings will pass, and brighter, impactful days are on the horizon. The good days will outweigh the challenging days.

I recall as a school principal, there were days that were challenging. Days that made me rethink, redesign and reposition myself in the role as the school leader. A leadership-learned lesson is to be optimistic and use challenging days to be grateful for all the good things that occurred and will continue to transpire.

I cannot imagine what my leadership would be like if I would have taken the path less travelled. For one to really know what they are truly made of and how great of a leader they are, I believe that they must face situations that will cause them to expand and extend themselves beyond what they think is humanly possible! They must go face to face with the inner foundation of their being and find a stable place within to navigate while serving as a leader.

There may be many days in which one may question their leadership abilities and wonder if they are meant to be a leader. Some of the most common questions posed are: Can I address another issue? Can I face another encounter? Can I do one more thing? Can I continue to make an impact? Can I have another critical conversation? Can I encourage others? Can I give more of my time? Can I extend myself beyond what I have already done? Can I deal with another crisis? Can I keep up with this pace? Can I build this team? Can I make changes that are sustainable? Can I grow and develop along with fulfilling these responsibilities? Can I do the job and do it well? Can I continue to be the example I desire to be to others? Can I keep the vision moving forward? Can I make sure we are abiding by the mission? Can the team meet its goals? Can we serve in unity? Can we make a powerful impact? Can we do what others believe cannot be done?

Of course, the questions can go on and on, but remember at the end of the day, it is the person in the mirror looking back at you who must answer the questions and move the organization forward. You have taken the oath to serve as the leader. Now, march and move forward in giving back and in serving with passion!

At this point, you are probably wondering if your leadership journey has crafted you into the leader you are today or if you were born with those specific traits. Again, I invite you to embrace the fact that you were molded into the leader you are now! You were designed to address all the complexities of being a dynamic leader. A leader who can withstand the unthinkable. A leader who can navigate the most challenging situations. A leader who can bring about the most impactful change during the most difficult times. You will need wisdom and advice from those who have taken the journey before you. You will need strength, hindsight, insight, foresight, practical application and skills that will allow you to bring about positive changes in the place that you are serving.

My first leadership experience allowed me to learn about the type of leader I was and the leader I was becoming. This was my platform to hone my skills and abilities, to utilize my strengths and learn about areas of growth. I made mistakes and learned by trial and error. Some of the lessons laid the groundwork for what would become my greatest asset. That is, my ability to transform schools into better learning institutions for students who were highly impacted. This skill has been a tremendous asset to my career. No matter the task or the assignment, I took advantage of every opportunity to grow my skills and develop my abilities. A lesson learned here is to embrace every opportunity and allow it to teach you something that will add to your leadership toolkit.

I had to learn not only how to be a leader, but learn how to be an *effective leader* who had to make significant improvements to the organization. Anytime you encounter massive challenges, you will either fold as a leader or you will embrace those monumental challenges and allow them to create the exemplified version of you! The tasks I encountered were massive, but my desire to overcome them was even greater.

Another lesson learned is to know what you are truly passionate about before deciding to commit to a position of leadership. If you serve with passion, you will be able to navigate your way with a certain sense of conviction. You will have a strong sense of dedication, a sense of a growth mindset, and a sense that no matter the challenge, you will succeed—not only in serving as a leader, but in extending your leadership capacity.

Amazingly, when you seek challenging growth opportunities, it has the tendency to create the best version of you. It allows you to use failures to groom for greatness. Sometimes, failures will bring out the best in you and you will learn so much about yourself and your abilities. You will learn things that cause you to accelerate your love to lead. You will also learn about things that will make you question your future desire to continue to serve. The first year in my role as a school leader, we did not make the kind of growth that I wanted us to make; but that process allowed me to build upon the small successes that led to the bigger successes. The lesson in all of this is to let the best of you evolve into the greatest version of you, and the biggest failures can become your greatest gains.

Another one of my leadership opportunities allowed me to expand my other set of skills that I never knew existed. I was able to tap into some of these hidden skills, explore some of the unknowns about me, hone my abilities, and learn about my untapped leadership skills. If I did not seek the opportunity and allowed fear to halt my decision, I would not be the leader I am today. Thank goodness I paid attention to my intuition and embrace the opportunities to expand and extend. Thank goodness I went into schools where others saw as failures, but I saw as opportunities to make an impact. The lesson is to let go of fear and step into unknown territories to discover your hidden potentials.

Leaders are known for motivating and encouraging other people to work towards achieving a common objective. They inspire, uplift and expand others to extend their capacity and align their actions to impact the overall vision of the organization. These are indeed some of the things that you should strive for while serving in this role.

Effective leaders possess a set of skills that are beneficial not only for themselves, but for the good of everyone involved. They continuously look for ways to elevate their knowledge and their skills. This lesson is a must in your toolkit.

Furthermore, leaders must possess a wide range of skills to accomplish the many tasks at hand. They must know how to effectively delegate to those who can assist the organization in achieving their goals. They should understand the managerial and operational aspects of their role and know how to create a winning team who can positively impact all involved and make a systemic difference.

We all know that leadership goes beyond just managing others. A leader must be able to manage resources, involve others, communicate effectively, motivate and inspire others, supervise others and help others to improve their skills. I had many years of experience not only leading others, but managing all aspects of schools to make them better! A valuable lesson is to learn from others while you are working to maximize your own skills and abilities.

There are leaders who ended up being great but did not appear to have the trait of "born to be a leader." I think of Steve Jobs who faced many challenges before becoming one of the most iconic leaders of all times. He made his mark and his legacy continues. There is a lot to learn from his journey.

During my time of serving as a leader, I have learned that leaders possess skills that encompass creativity and innovation. They know how to share the responsibilities with others in the organization and others feel empowered when this is the natural way of operating. A sense of accountability must be embedded, and leaders must show integrity and honesty. Their ability to inspire others, their commitment and passion for serving, and their ability to communicate with others are all important to the DNA of a great leader! Once a leader has served for a while, they begin to understand their leadership style, their traits and how they operate within the context of the organizations.

Based on the many years I served as leader, I was able to identify my leadership style. It is being a transformational leader. I found this out early on in my leadership career. I continue to serve in that capacity while making an impact in transforming the minds, the skills, and the desire that others have in serving.

In my role as a transformational leader, I had to create a vision so that others could embrace and motivate themselves to serve at their highest level of service. I had to make sure they were engaged in the process, and create protocols and structure so that everyone could maximize their individual skills while working collectively to master objectives. Effective leaders know how to merge the skills of everyone to positively impact the organization.

There are many overarching lessons that I learned throughout my journey that allowed me to be an award-winning leader. Those strategies I continue to share are: be realistic in your approach no matter what situation you go into; think about where you aspire to be in the end and create strategies to help you reach the goals you set forth; make sure you provide direction to others and set priorities that will elevate you to what you are striving to achieve. Always do what you love, and love what you do and realize that this is "*Hard* work, but also *heart* work!" Leaders tend to operate in a proactive manner, possess great problem-solving skills and develop a grand vision that is compelling.

As I reflect over my career and all the outstanding leaders I have met, I realize they told inspiring stories that would capture your attention and make you gravitate towards their leadership style. They created something that was meaningful, and people would want to follow them from organization to organization. I, too, experienced this in my years of serving.

Another important noted attribute of great leaders was their ability to create other leaders within the organization. I, too, contribute this to a lot of my own success. I allowed leaders to navigate in their own way and they were able to make our organization better due to their own set of strengths and their skillsets. I would always tell my employees that when you come into this organization, I do not want the visitors to be able to tell who the leader is in the organization, but for everyone to be a strong leader. Amazingly, they would shine every time. This is another lesson I pass on to you. Allow others to be as important as you and wear the title of teamwork, team pride and team attitude.

Finally, I invite you to continue the journey of serving, honing your skills, exploring the unknowns about your leadership style, and impacting others. Be enthusiastic in developing into a great leader and keep people connected to the vision. Serve from the heart and impact the minds! Always give back and make a profound difference! This will ensure your success and will help you to elevate your aspirations while being in one of the most rewarding positions - *leadership*!

Reflection Questions:

1) Now that you have read the chapter, what are the lessons that you can apply to your own leadership?
2) What are you passionate about and how have you aligned this passion to your own leadership style?
3) What are you currently doing to elevate your knowledge and extend your skills?

Alandes Powell

I communicate what I expect of others, clearly and concisely.

The True Meaning of Authentic Leadership

As I sat in the boardroom, which held approximately 17 people, I looked around the room. On this particular day, I felt the loneliness that comes with being the only black person in the room more than usual. I had grown quite accustomed to being the only one at the table when I traveled to meet peers, partners and leaders from around the U.S. Yes, I used black to describe myself. I realize that most people think the best term is African-American, but my preference is black. I think it makes a more profound statement.

So, I felt a little more alone. As my youngest son said once after being the only black at a party, I felt "a little more black than normal." I felt justified since it was the first day we'd all met since the election—you know, *the* election. Not the election that made black Americans smile with pride and honor. Not the one that made us feel like we finally belonged in America. Not the one that made blacks nationwide feel as though our country had finally progressed. Nope, not that election. *The other one.* The one that did just the opposite. But, as the day went on, I remembered why I was sitting there and how I got there. More importantly, I remembered my role as a black female sitting at a corporate table.

I thought, *This is what authentic leadership is all about—no, not being black, but being true.* True to who you are and what you think. True to your voice echoing what others may shy away from saying, or giving others the opportunity to think about how decisions may impact people from all walks of life. So, I pushed it off and said to myself, "This is just another leadership test that I hope and pray I will pass." Up until this point, not one person had mentioned the election. We were on two days post-election, and no one even brought up the potential upside to corporate America of having *him* in office. I still couldn't shake the feeling, the uneasiness. Maybe it was the silence regarding such a big event that wrecked my nerves.

Mid-afternoon on the second day of the meeting, I left to jump on a conference call. While away, I received a text from a co-worker that read: *The moment you left the room, everyone started having a love fest for the new president.*

I replied, *You have to be kidding me!*

She said, *Nope! They are all excited and singing his praises.* I wondered as I finished my meeting why I felt so upset because of her note. Was it because they had waited until I left the room, or was it the fact that they were excited that I felt betrayed? Before returning to the room, I said my normal quick prayer, asking God to grant me wisdom, to help me never take things personally, and to cover my mouth.

The room immediately fell quiet as I entered. Knowing what had just been discussed made me notice everyone's body language. It was as if I had just walked in and caught one of my kids doing something they had no business doing. As I sat down, a person decided to be *authentic*.

She said, "I don't know why the media keeps portraying him as awful or racist. He is not. It's just the media."

I watched as a few people looked in shock while others looked at me with a look of sympathy. Now I was pissed. I don't believe leaders should ever act or be viewed as victims. I'm not saying no one does leaders wrong. But acting or being treated as a victim just doesn't align with the character traits of a leader. I decided to let it go, but she just wouldn't stop. She repeated it. That's when I decided I needed to handle this right the first time.

It took me approximately two or three seconds to decide what to say. When I did, I said, "Everyone has a viewpoint. But, quite honestly, I am having a hard time understanding how people I have come to respect and consider genuine friends were okay with putting my family at risk. I can't understand why people can't see or feel what I am feeling. So, I am trying to keep holding on to the fact we are all different and we all have the right to see things through our own eyes. This includes the media, which is also made up of people."

Authentic leadership consists of building honest relationships with an ethical foundation. My belief is that the application of authentic leadership is how the person defines it, and it is personal in nature. Being authentic means holding people accountable for their words and ensuring that my voice is true to what I believe. It means delivering my message in a constructive, clear and concise manner, which creates win-wins for all involved. I have learned this through my mistakes and whenever I have failed to speak up in a timely manner. The essence of true authentic leadership is seeing things through your eyes but remaining open to hearing others viewpoint and being willing to change, when necessary.

There have been times when I have handled these types of matters with silence, which made matters worse. I would often go home feeling defeated. I felt phony. I felt like I was failing others who depended on my voice, my insight, my integrity and my transparency. I learned this lesson the hard way, and it was a lesson that I keep in my heart, which provides me the fuel needed to always speak up. Another leader, referred to me as "The Ghetto Director" whenever we were in leadership meetings. I would smile, but I was upset on the inside. During this time, I failed to think that he might think it was okay to talk to other people that way, specifically Black people. I never felt like his intent was ugly, but his words didn't make me feel good.

One day, I told my husband, "If he says it again, I'm going to pull him aside and explain how it made me feel and let him know that it was extremely inappropriate."

The next day during a meeting with over 700 people, he introduced me to the crowd as "The Ghetto Director" and I felt like passing out. Instead, I stood there and spoke to the group with all the energy I could muster. Then, I quickly retreated to my office. It took me some time to recover from that one. The mistake was costly to him, and it taught me the real meaning of being true to myself and my feelings. It taught me the importance of using my authentic voice.

As a leader, when you fail to speak up, when you fail to provide your truth and use your voice, you potentially negatively impact people and your organization. Sharing your truth in a manner that is respectful and transparent, and maintaining an openness to listen and change, is what makes others follow you. This is what helps bring out your greatness. Silence can be harmful, especially when you allow decisions to be made, or things to be said, that will possibly be perceived differently by others. It is unfair to others when you don't speak up. As authentic leaders, we must always operate with courage, integrity and wisdom. We must be willing to help others change and we must be just as willing to be changed. Your goal must be to become better while making the people around you better.

As leaders, we must also learn from other leaders. When someone shows you greatness, you can't help but respond and follow them.

Years ago when my boss gave me a performance review that I vehemently didn't agree with, I was extremely vocal about it. I felt like he actually considered one of my weaknesses to be a strength and one of my strengths as a weakness. Although it would have been easy for me to just focus on my strengths, I provided examples of both. We continued to work together, and, within a few months, he came to me with different feedback.

"You were right," he said. "Leadership is your strength, but you do need to work on your communication style with your peers." Just like that, we became mentee and mentor. Over the years, we became friends and our relationship helped me to grow as a leader and a person. We are still friends today, and he has helped open many doors for me that may have remain closed otherwise. Because I was honest about both my strengths and opportunities, he trusted me with large roles and responsibilities throughout my career. It all went back to how he was able to acknowledge when he was wrong and how I trusted him.

In leadership, it is just as important to follow as it is to lead. I have learned so much from others, even those leaders who I once considered "questionable." Back up your words with your actions. People believe what they see more than what they hear. Allowing people to feel your heart, helping them understand your values, and walking in the path that encompasses all of you is the definition of true transparent leadership. We must be okay with failing at times but recover quickly. Brush yourself off and get back out there.

Musts of Leadership

- Leaders must always act with integrity and courage.
- Leaders must plan to give more than they expect to receive.
- Leaders must be willing to walk ahead of others and look around the corner to make sure it is safe before bringing others in--all the while, making others feel as though they are walking right beside them.
- Leaders cannot be both victim and leader.
- Leaders must motivate others.
- Leaders must inspire through connections of stories, events and viewpoints.
- Leaders must be willing to sacrifice, when necessary.
- Leaders must operate with compassion.
- Leaders must have the courage to take action and the courage to allow it to hurt.

Questions

1. What are your three "musts" of leadership?
2. What are the most useful resources you would recommend to someone looking to gain a better perspective on becoming a better leader?
3. What's one key leadership lesson you have learned along the way?

Jaresha Moore

*I am soaring to success by empowering
my daily growth to be a great leader.*

Empowering Your Inner Leader

I will never forget the day that I was called into the CEO's office of a previous employer. I was told that I was doing such an exceptional job leading the team that I was being promoted to business manager. My first thought was, *How amazing is it that they truly see my value and recognize the great work that I have been doing for the last four years?* The next thought made that first thought disappear. It was as if it had never popped into my mind. I could understand why, but all I kept thinking was, *"How? How am I going to lead this team? I don't have any experience managing a team. What if I don't do a good job leading the team? What if I fail as a new leader?"* So much self-doubt and negativity clouded my mind that I questioned whether or not I could actually do the job.

What I didn't realize then is that my first experience as a new leader and manager opened the door to opportunities and learning experiences that I never knew existed within myself. I had a choice to make. I could tell my boss and CEO that I appreciated the opportunity and offer, but I just didn't think I was ready to be the manager of the team—or, I could do it afraid, step out of my comfort zone and empower my inner leader.

Empower Your Inner Leader

To lead effectively, a leader must first know how to lead himself. For a leader to know how to lead himself, he must know and understand *why* it's important to empower your inner leader. Being a leader comes with great responsibility. A leader cannot lead anyone else until they have taken the steps to lead themselves. However, leaders are leading every single day. Some are leading who probably shouldn't be leading because they didn't take the necessary steps to empower their inner leader. They didn't learn how to lead themselves first.

Great leaders understand how important it is to empower and to lead "self" first before attempting to lead and influence others. Great leaders also understand that being a great leader means committing to empowering and investing in people to help them reach their highest potential. For this to happen, each leader must recognize where they are, where they are trying to go, and how they plan to get there. If you don't know where you are as a leader, you can't move to the next level. As a result, I discovered that to empower your inner leader, you have to ask yourself some key questions.

1. Where are you?

Although I had several doubts about being a new leader, I knew that I was so excited to be able to continue supporting the team as a manager. However, I recognized that I needed to grow and develop as a new leader. In life, we don't know what we don't know. However, it is our job to discover and learn to excel in life. Being promoted gave me the push that I needed to empower myself for growth and success. It allowed me to take a look at my goals, and it helped me develop the skills needed to move forward as a new leader.

2. Where are you trying to go?

Great leaders never stop learning and growing. The great thing about asking, "Where are you trying to go?" is that you never stop asking this question, no matter what level you reach as a leader. I wanted to be a great leader. However, I had to gain clarity on *where* I truly wanted to go and *why*. I knew that I wanted to invest in my team and to empower them to reach their personal and professional goals. Why was this so important to me, though? It was so important because I wanted to see them accomplish their goals. I wanted each person on the team to feel valued and appreciated.

3. How do you plan to get there?

Growth is a process. It doesn't happen overnight. New leaders need to set S.M.A.R.T. (Smart, Measurable, Attainable, Realistic, Time-bound) goals and D.U.M.B. (Dream-driven, Uplifting, Motivated and Bold) goals. Leaders must also develop action steps to help them grow as a leader. Before I was promoted, I invested in all kinds of self-development books and programs. After the promotion, I became obsessed with self-development programs. I also searched for leadership conferences, webinars and workshops to help me develop as a leader.

Additionally, I had a great accountability coach who supported me through the process. A wise person once said, "You want to go fast, go alone. If you want to go far, go together." As a new leader, he needs a mentor and/or boss who will support him on his journey. The amazing thing for me was that I had a great boss who invested in me and held me accountable for growing as a leader.

After asking yourself these three great questions to help empower your inner leader, it doesn't stop there. When I started leading many years ago, I was determined not to listen to the inner voice, self-doubt and limiting beliefs that told me I was too young to lead. I didn't know what I was doing, and no one would ever take me seriously as a leader. I began to empower my inner leader, and I knew I had to S.O.A.R. N.O.W.

If there is nothing else that you learn from this chapter, please remember that as a leader, you will be pushed out of your comfort zone. There will be many tasks that you will have to do that will make you feel uncomfortable. But remember, people are watching and learning. S.O.A.R N.O.W. (Empower Strength, Create Opportunities, Innovate Aspiration, Achieve Results, Next Move, Ongoing Actions, Win on Purpose) is a strategy that I created to help myself and others grow as leaders. After gaining clarity on where I was, where I was trying to go, and how I plan to get there, these actionable steps helped me grow as a leader.

Similar to an eagle, as a new leader, you start on the ground and prepare yourself for take-off. Then, you fly up and go higher. Then, when you're ready, you spread your wings like an eagle and soar. As a new leader, you start on the ground and must empower yourself to reach the next level by developing. As you develop and grow, and you ascend by continuing to empower yourself to empower others, you fly higher and higher. To soar, it takes practice and development to reach a point where you can S.O.A.R. N.O.W. For me as a new leader, S.O.A.R. N.O.W. was what I needed to take me from feeling stuck in discovering my place as a new leader, to feeling confident enough to spread my wings and soar as a leader to empower myself and my team.

Empower Your Strength

I remember attending one of the first meetings that I was asked to chair after being promoted. The energy was so negative in the room, I could feel anger and resentment so strongly that it felt like I had a freshly brewed cup of coffee. I could have allowed this to intimidate me. It was clear that everyone in the room had their agenda, and no one wanted to hear anything that I had to discuss.

However, I politely called the meeting to order and started off by addressing the elephant in the room. I redirected the negative energy to positive energy and got right to the point for the meeting. After the meeting, one of the ladies pulled me to the side.

"You did a great job organizing the meeting and keeping everyone focused on the task at hand," she said. "In the past, these meetings have been all over the place. I think you being the new business manager is going to be a great thing for the team and organization."

As a leader, it is important to know your strengths and weaknesses. Then, empower them. Write down all of your qualities, strengths and weaknesses, and use this list to help you grow as a leader. Ask yourself, "As a leader, how can I use my strengths to help me lead today? How can I use my weaknesses to help me learn today?"

Create Opportunities

One of the keys to being a great leader is knowing that every day is another day that you can create opportunities for growth. When you become a leader, the first thing all want to do is be a best and greatest leader as though you wait for someone to hand you the certificate of greatest. Greatness doesn't happen overnight. It takes work. You may have to try something and fail the first time. It takes time and effort to become great. Make sure you are intentional about creating those opportunities for growth.

When I first started leading, I had so many ideas of how I wanted things to improve for my team. However, I knew there were some areas that I needed to improve for myself first. For example, there was a particular system that one of my employees had to use to input invoices. She was the only one who knew how to use the system. Therefore, I went through the training to learn the system. I also wanted to understand some of the challenges and frustrations she went through when using the system. In this case, I was able to learn some of the ins and outs since it was a smaller company.

However, as leaders, you're not growing as a leader if your team is performing a task that you can't identify with on any level. There may be an opportunity for you to grow and learn more as a leader to help your team. Another example would be attending a leadership conference and having a meeting with your team after to share what you learned from the conference. How are you creating growth opportunities for you to become a better leader?

Innovate Aspiration

Every day that you jump in the car to travel to work, I'm sure you don't have to plug your work address into your GPS to get there. You automatically know what streets to turn on to get to your destination. You know how long it's going to take you to get there. As a great leader, you are on a journey that requires innovation and aspiration to keep you growing and moving. Great leaders are visionaries with big ideas. They motivate and influence other people to create big ideas and dreams.

John Maxwell states, "Good leaders must communicate vision clearly, creatively and continually. However, the vision doesn't come alive until the leader models it."

When I became a leader in healthcare, I recognized that I got promoted to a job that required me to incorporate "innovate-aspiration." I used my skills and strengths in process improvement to generate big ideas. I incorporated processes that I implemented first to show the team how it could potentially help them become more effective and more efficient. Leaders come up with great ideas every day, but many don't do anything with those ideas. As a leader, what is your strategy or plan to put innovate-aspiration into action to grow and model as a leader?

Achieve Results

Successful leaders set goals that are measurable and achievable. To develop as a leader, it is important to set those personal goals for yourself to help empower your inner leader. When I started as a leader, I didn't realize how important it was to set measurable and achievable goals. I thought I could set huge goals without a measurable plan of action. Then I wondered why I had a hard time getting results. I had to learn the hard way. I realized from a mentor that I was setting myself up for failure. It was important to set goals, but it was equally important to be able to achieve them to keep growing as a leader. What goals are you setting for the team that you're not achieving as a leader? Do you need to reevaluate your goals to make sure you can measure your success?

Next Move

When I became a new manager, I did an inventory of what was working for the department and what needed to be improved. Just as it's important to make this list for the department, it is important to make the list for yourself. As a leader, make an inventory of the areas that you have grown in and the areas in which you need to improve. Always write down the next move or next steps for each of the areas. Some suggested areas could be personal/professional, relationships, finances, health and fitness, and spiritual. There should always be a next move for you to make. As a leader, what is the next move that you need to take or make to grow?

Ongoing Actions

Ongoing actions keep you focused on the next move and the actions that you need to take to continue to grow and empower your inner leader. Once you determine what your next move is, it's time to focus on the continued actions to keep growing. As a leader, what actions will you take after you decide your next move?

Win On Purpose

Years ago, I was given the opportunity to become a new leader. I could have decided to sit back, wait and hope that, one day, I would be a successful leader. Or, I could go out and learn to grow and develop my inner leader. Every day, we have a choice to do nothing or to win on purpose.

To win, you have to know the rules to play. Then, you have to think and win like a champion. As a leader, are you winning on purpose on your growth journey?

Use S.O.A.R. N.O.W daily to help you take intentional, actionable steps to develop and grow as a leader. At the beginning of each workday, ask yourself these questions:

1. How can you use S.O.A.R N.O.W. to be a successful leader and make an impact today?

2. Who can you share S.O.A.R. N.O.W with to help them become a better leader?

3. What kind of leader are you hoping to become as a result of S.O.A.R N.O.W?

Apply the strategies and take time to pause and reflect at the end of each work week to see how you were able to S.O.A.R N.O.W. Remember, practice makes permanent and empowerment builds leaders.

Maya Dorsey

My relationships with people will

influence the success of my work.

Your Relationships Will Sustain You

So you think you're ready? Every graduate walks across that stage after years of hard work, ready to take on the world. Just because you've graduated and you have a degree doesn't automatically make you "ready." Even with the degree, you may be missing some key components to be a successful leader.

"I've learned that people will forget what you said, people will forget what you did, but people will never forget how you made them feel."

~Maya Angelou

This chapter is meant to help you reflect on critical components of leadership. Its purpose is to help you recognize that investing time in building healthy connections with people is the first step in yielding positive outcomes. The quote by Maya Angelou rings true in any setting. We shouldn't be more focused on the goal than we are on the people and the relationships that are essential to deliver those goals.

Eager and Ready to Change the World

Relationship building is true in all industries, but it is especially true in education, where we aren't interacting with a product, but *people*. I've witnessed novice educators fresh out of college start their new teaching jobs, eager and revved up to change the world. Isn't that why we do it? The newness of the first days wear off quickly. You've learned your students' names and you've practiced your schedules for a couple of weeks. Now the *real* work starts. Teachers often make the mistake of viewing themselves as the "experts" and often assume that the students are lucky to learn from them. This idea creates distance between the teacher and their students because teachers don't always allow themselves to be open to learn from their students.

Relationship Takeaway #1- Relationships Matter

In my first year of teaching in public school, I had three years of prior teaching experience under my belt. I had previous teaching from a charter school. Plus, I served as a substitute for a couple of years in local school districts, too. I had mastered the art of making beautiful bulletin boards and creating a theme around a catchy phrase. The room was beautiful! I thought I was ready for the students. *This would be no different than the rest of my teaching experience,* I thought to myself.

My pretty room meant nothing after the first few weeks of school. I surveyed the room at the end of one particular school day, and I noticed letters missing on the "beautiful" bulletin board with my catchy slogans. My border was hanging on by a staple, *literally*. At that moment, I realized that I'd been focused on the wrong things. My first couple of weeks shouldn't have only been concentrated on beautifying my room. Those weeks shouldn't have been focused on setting routines and procedures. Instead, I should have put the majority of my energy into building authentic relationships with my students and their families. I should have saved the couple hundred dollars I spent on matching the border with the name tags and bulletin boards. I should have waited until the school year started and allowed the students to help set up *our* room. Their art work, stories and ideas should have littered the boards. I realized that they had absolutely no buy-in into how I had designed *my* classroom. Knowing what I know now, I would certainly do things differently.

I learned a valuable lesson that school year. A couple years later, a novice teacher joined our wing. She was fresh out of college. She was glad to have her first "real" teaching job. She was young and white, and she lived in a rural community nearby. She was excited to "teach." I watched as her initial excitement, which flew as high as a kite in August, swiftly lost its height within the first couple of months of that school year. Daily, I heard her screaming and blowing whistles. Yet, she still didn't gain the respect of her students. Many days, she stormed out of her classroom, crying and threatening to quit.

She was guilty of making the same mistake I made: not taking the time to build relationships first. She was so focused on doing things equally rather than with equity. Equity means recognizing that we are all in need of something. Many times, those *somethings* are different. When you take the time to build authentic relationships, you learn where people come from, how they tick and how they tock. You learn their strengths and their weaknesses. A good leader uses that communication and takes the time to develop and empower in those areas.

No matter what your profession is, you must examine your environment before starting anything. It's important to put your finger on the pulse of the culture. You must get a sense of the environment before spewing your *great ideas*! Your degree may have helped you get the job, but in order to do the job well, you must develop positive relationships with your staff and the people you serve. Leaders often make the mistake of putting pressure on themselves to know *everything*. Stop! Give yourself the permission *not* to have all of the answers. Be honest with your colleagues and staff by simply saying, "I don't have the answer to that, but I'll find out." It makes you "normal" and it earns you much more respect than barking orders at others as though you have it all together. John Maxwell said, "The greatest mistake we make is living in constant fear that we will make one." It is important to become a student of your work. Choosing to model being a learner is encouraging. It inspires those around you to be open-minded and they are more willing to do the same.

Relationship Takeaway #2- Learn While You Lead

After finishing my second master's degree in educational leadership, I was eager to wrap up my whole experience with my administrator's license. But first, I had to conquer the task of passing the test. I completed the program, so I thought surely getting my license would be a cinch. Well, it wasn't. After about the fifth attempt, my frustration ballooned. One by one, I witnessed my fellow classmates celebrate the passing of their tests. I was thinking to myself, *We took the same courses. How are they passing and I am not?*

Over the years, working in my then school district, I made several good friends who were already administrators. One day, I vented to one of my admin friends about my failed attempts. I asked her if she had any study materials for me. She had taken the test a few years prior. Unfortunately, since then, the testing vendor had changed. It was a whole new test. She gave me some pointers from what she recalled from her test. Well, I listened and I still didn't pass it.

I shared my continuous disappointment with her and I was completely drained by it. She saw my frustration and said, "I'm going to take the test!"

I looked up at her and said, "How?"

She replied, "I am going to sign up and go take the test."

I thought, *No way! She's just saying this to make me feel better.* I knew she meant well and I knew she was a good person. But, I thought she would be too busy and wouldn't be able to do it. After all, it wasn't hers to take. She had her license. But sure enough, she registered and took the time to take a three-hour test. Afterwards, we debriefed and she shared how she could see the potential challenges. The test results came back a few weeks later and she'd passed. I was completely grateful that she took the time and her money to invest in helping me. Now that's what you call "putting your money where your mouth is!" She proved that she had my back and that she wanted to see me succeed. That investment made me continue to fight to pass the test. It took a few more times before I passed on the ninth try. Had I not had this relationship, maybe I wouldn't have been so motivated to keep at it. While I knew people were rooting against me, I further knew that I had people rooting for me.

Joe Clark Days Are Over! Rethinking How to Lead

Everyone is familiar with the acclaimed film, *Lean on Me*. The character, Joe Clark, portrayed by Morgan Freeman, was a no-nonsense principal who was called in to clean up a school by any means necessary. The problem with his style of leadership was that he was a one-man show. He was a dictator, and he led by fear and intimidation. Did he care about the kids? Yes, he did. But could he get the results he wanted alone? No! The sustainable changes that Joe wanted to make couldn't be maintained long-term. Joe's autocratic leadership style pushed people away from him, ultimately hurting the culture of the school. The assistant principal confronted him regarding the way she and the other staff members felt like they'd been mistreated and she threatened to resign. Joe got it together. He realized that he needed to foster better relationships with his staff. He started to see them as teammates rather than opponents.

Relationship Takeaway #3- Develop Quality Relationships with People Who Can Stretch You

My former principal, Mrs. Croker, was a tough-as-nails leader with a deep love for students. I would describe her as an iron hand in a velvet glove. What made her different from Joe Clark was that she was great at knowing her *who*. She watched people like an eagle. She saw others when they didn't see her. She believed in putting people to work. She examined people and got a sense quickly of people's strengths and weaknesses. If you were open, she coached you to become better. But if you wanted to stay stuck, she didn't mind having the conversation that maybe this isn't the right fit for you. I was fortunate that she saw leadership qualities in me. She took the time to build a relationship with me. Through that relationship, I, too, would be subject to some tough conversations. She challenged me to be my best. She wasn't accepting anything else from me. I had a lot to learn. I am grateful that she was not only my principal, but also my mentor. I credit her for a lot of the reason why I am a leader today. She saw something in me and put in the "sweat equity," as she would call it, to ensure that I had the tools to be successful. She showed me how to lead with compassion, without compromising my *why*.

My *why* was to make a difference in the lives of students. She ingrained in me to never lose sight of the *why*. The *why* was, and is, the driving force for everything. I watched how she collaborated with her assistant principals. They were a team. I watched how she empowered them to lead and make decisions. She was a model for teamwork and used it to make a difference. During her tenure, grade level teams were stronger. People were relational. Communication was frequent and teamwork was present. The students knew it, too. They understood that they couldn't misspeak on the behalf of their teacher. The teachers were united and transparent about needs. They were willing to support each other through challenges in an effort for everyone to be successful. It wasn't perfect. There were some people who didn't want to buy-in to the "kumbaya" environment. Because the leader was intentional, consistent and relational, there were more people who bought into it than those who did not.

I Got the Power!

The notion that the leader holds the sole power is completely untrue. You may be the head, but the people are the neck. You cannot make change without having buy-in from the team. So in actuality, the power belongs to the people. Having a title doesn't make you a leader. Being willing to roll your sleeves up and work alongside your team is the true display of leadership. It is important to listen more and talk less. Listening should be one of the greatest assets of a leader. It's important to make time to hear what people are thinking and consider their suggestions.

People are hired because someone believes they can get the job done. The more you take the time to connect with people, the more relational trust is built. When trust is established, it lends to a better flow of communication. Communication is vital to the success of any great team. Jada Pinkett Smith says, "My belief is that communications is the best way to create strong relationships."

Strong relationships are vital to long-term success as it develops a mutual respect between you and your team. It also helps to open the aperture of the leader, providing insight on what grinds people's gears. This equips the leader with the knowledge of the best methods of communication to use with individuals and/or teams. It is important for people to view their leader as someone who empowers them rather than someone who dictates to them. When good relationships are established, it is easier to digest corrective feedback.

Relationship Takeaways

All leaders need to have powerful, authentic relationships to help them excel in their career. Quite frankly, no one knows it all. When you think about relationship capital, these three tidbits should come to mind. First, relationships do matter. Take the time to create authentic relationships. It is essential and it communicates value. Secondly, learn while you lead. You should be coachable, too. Be willing to be a student of your work. Continue to challenge yourself to grow. Reflect on your practices and how you can continue to broaden your leadership skills. Thirdly, develop quality relationships with people who can stretch you. Leaders need mentors, too. Find someone who may be successful in areas you need to strengthen or would like to know more about. Leadership can be tough, but also very rewarding. The good news is that you don't have to do it alone. If you master these simple lessons, it will help you balance the scales of your leadership—leaving you more motivated.

"We are not a team because we work together. We are a team because we respect, trust and care for each other."

~Vala Afshar

"Nothing will work unless you do."

~Maya Angelou

"If you do what you've always done, you'll get what you've always gotten."

~ Tony Robbins

As you prepare for your leadership relationship journey, think about these five questions:

1. How do I build relational trust?

2. Who do I have in my professional circle who stretches me?

3. What is my relationship messaging to my team?

4. Why are relationships important in my role?

5. Do I share the role of leadership?

Natalie Ocean Canty

I believe, trust and have confidence that this is my best.

Is Image Really Everything?

"Bring Your Best Self into Every Situation and Trust
That You Are Prepared For The Moment"

My mother always required more from me. Something about the way she looked at me, said my name and questioned my decisions, gave me pause that she expected more from me. She restricted me from getting a perm at ten years old. She didn't allow me to be out past sunset, and I could never miss Sunday School. All of these (and many other) restrictions contributed to shaping my character and self-image. But, as the years passed, I realized that I had to require more of myself. So, as I ponder the question, "Is image really everything?", I must respond with a resounding, "Yes!" Image *is* everything—when it has been defined, developed, packaged, refined and then packaged again.

Self-Image Defined

Oftentimes when we consider self-image, we focus on what we are wearing, how defined our makeup is, what shoes we are wearing (and the condition of our shoes), and how well our hair is groomed. These are exterior necessities for making a good first impression. First impressions have an important place in presenting our full package to others. However, as we consider the work we do to ensure our exterior impression is sharp, we must also align with the rejection of subpar actions that follow. We underperform in meetings or our work. We are late for everything. We only have relationships that benefit us—despite the fact that healthy relationships should be mutually beneficial.

I define *self-image* as my total self being presented to others to leave an impression that describes who I am. The imprint of my image should make people see roses and lily fields after I have left their presence. I want to positively impact others when I encounter them.

Reflect on the Foundation of Your Self-Image

The foundation of my self-image was shaped by my mother,

grandparents, senior women at church, teachers, my neighbors and my peers. This foundation was filled with love, positive confirmations and negative statements. It was up to me to let the positive trample over the negative. I have been the same height since fifth grade—5'4". So, you can imagine how school went until I got to ninth grade (which gave most kids time to grow). My self-image took a hit because I was the second tallest person in class. I was always asked to stand in the back of the line and sit in the back of the class. I was always asked to reach all the items on the top shelf. In retrospect, this also meant that I was not picked on a lot by my peers. I rarely got into fights and teachers always knew me. It didn't hurt that I had a unique last name. Now this retrospective moment was as an adult, not as the eleven-year-old who was tall and feeling awkward in grade school.

As an eleven-year-old, I had to quickly put on tough skin to be able to handle all the jokes and ridicules. I also became an avid reader and used my vocabulary words to attack people. The balance for me came from attending Sunday School and hearing lessons that lifted my self-confidence. Those lessons reassured me that there was purpose for my life, even if I was the second tallest kid in school.

What has happened in our past shapes our current perspective and strongly contributes to our future activity. We must decide what impact we will let each situation contribute to our future success.

Here are a few self-reflecting questions:

- What was the foundation of your self-image?
- Have you ever stopped to ask yourself, "What (or whom) has shaped my self-image?"
- Why do you perform the way that you do?
- What type of people do you attract?
- What type of relationships do you maintain?

Take a few moments to answer these questions. It will help you determine the elements that have shaped the person you have become today and will guide you toward the person you want to become. You cannot go through life just winging it and making mistakes that are supposed to correct themselves. You cannot go through life in and out of relationships. You must ask yourself, "How much time I have spent preparing for *this* opportunity, job interview, relationship or promotion? What will my *next* look like?" Let's look at developing your image.

Developing Your Image

Your time is limited, so don't waste it living someone else's life.

~ Steven Jobs

When I was a little girl, I was always complimented on my long hair, pretty eyes and book smarts. I was noted for being tall. In junior high school, my science teacher got annoyed with me for being so talkative. I would do my work, then chat it up with anyone within earshot. I aggravated this teacher so much that he gave me two unsatisfactory marks in red under the soft skills side of my report card. He put them in bold red letters with exclamation points. I personally thought it was funny, but my mother thought differently.

I had no idea how my mother would respond, but I took the report card home and handed it to her. Besides, I had an 87 in the class. My mom looked at me and said, "If that's how you want to be remembered by your teachers, keep that behavior up. But I would suggest that you focus on getting your grade to a solid A and leave the chatterbox title to someone else." I didn't listen; I continued being chatty. I share this story because it is so easy to look in retrospect and see that my mom was trying to mentor me to better behavior that would have a more positive impact on my grade. But I missed it. I went through junior high school as a chatterbox. High school was a different place, so I changed my behavior. Besides, the rest of the students had caught up to my height! I only adjusted because the circumstances changed. I missed the point of autocorrecting in junior high.

It's important that we practice autocorrecting. *Autocorrecting* is when you think back over your response, attitude and appearance, and self-correct the errors that were made. Developing your image does not happen overnight. It will require deliberate action. As a matter of fact, it will take you a lifetime to perfect *you*. You can count on a mentor to advise you, but *you* must implement the necessary changes. Developing your image will include an honest assessment of where you are compared to where you want to end up. You must assess yourself at different times in life. If you desire to be a restaurant hostess, and your self-assessment shows that you lack capacity to be cordial to others, you either want to rethink your profession, or put the time in to practice being cordial to other people. Only practicing in a mirror by yourself will not give you the results you need. Once you have spent time practicing alone, you then need to practice on people who you do not know. Practicing on people who you know may give you a false sense of preparation. Strangers will respond to you with an honesty that those who know you may not have. Strangers will determine whether you have developed the desired skillset correctly. Once you have improved your image, master your many faces!

How Many Faces Do You Wear?

This above all: to thine own self be true!

~ William Shakespeare

Have you ever noticed that companies typically keep the same logo for decades, only with slight modifications over time? The same companies change their mission statement, but hold on to the vision statement. More recently, companies have begun to keep their mission and vision statements, and they simply add a core value statement. Our image is ever-evolving. The self-image I projected as a kid—smart, chatterbox—shifted when I became a young adult, then shifted again in my 30s and 40s. I believe the cause of this shifting is because of life changes that we experience as individuals.

Life changes force tweaks to our image. That's fine, as long as the alterations are improvements. You must be true to who you are always. Within that, you must be mindful of your surroundings. In one day, you may wear your mommy (or daddy) face, then shift to your supervisor face. A little later, you shift to the wife (or husband) face. The point here is that we all wear different faces, depending on the circumstances. One problem with our ever-changing responsibilities is knowing when to put on the right face. Have you ever stepped into a meeting and, to make yourself feel comfortable, you drop a joke to a coworker, who then proceeds to look at you as if you are crazy? The joke is not the problem (or perhaps it is). The issue is timing. You have on your "friend face" when you need to have on your "professional face." Honestly, this is where you must be able to read a room and/or a person to know which face you need to wear. I thought drinking a Coke would get me both many faces and a feeling of being refreshed. The lesson was much more substantive.

Owning Your Image

Happiness is when what you think, what you say,
and what you do are in harmony.

Mahatma Gandhi

Growing up, I was mesmerized with that infamous Coca-Cola commercial where they sang, "I'd like to teach the world to sing (in perfect harmony)." As a kid, the image I saw was that we live in a world where there are so many cultures and they all like Coca-Cola. Recently, I watched this commercial again. What I saw this time was the genius of marketing. Coca-Cola was sending a unifying message to the United States because, by July 8, 1971 (the day the commercial aired), our country was experiencing many layers of tumultuous times. As a brand, Coca-Cola was owning the unifying message. This commercial was created to rebrand Coca-Cola, which was founded on January 29, 1892. This felt like perhaps the first of many defining moments for Coca-Cola.

What has been your defining moment? Was it your first job interview? The first time you became a manager? The birth of your first child? When that defining moment happened, what was your image? Had you pulled it all together and were you operating at your A-game? Or were you just fumbling through? My defining moment came when I was in my thirties. I had decided in the seventh grade that, when I grew up, I wanted to be a secretary to a CEO, and this would take me my entire life to accomplish. I would work hard at it. Well, fast forward. My dream did not factor in a few things. I accomplished at 34 what I thought would take me a lifetime. The defining moment was when I realized that I had developed skills that pulled me out of the secretary pool. I had to rebrand myself and tweak my image.

You must own your image, which really means to have confidence that you are equipped to handle whatever comes next. The foundation of this confidence is a self-assessment of what skills you bring to the table, how you have performed to this point, and if your outward appearance matches the destiny you see for yourself. Once you have built this confidence, you can own *you*. In order to maintain your confidence, you must develop your own plan of best practices.

Best Practices

For some people, best practices include reading motivational books, self-help books, industry articles and novels. They may also attend networking events, motivational sessions and industry conferences. How you determine what your best practices will look like really depends on your industry. Certain industries require professionals to regularly sharpen their skills, including K-12 teachers, lawyers, accountants, bankers, doctors, nurses and skilled workers. For other industries, where continuing education is not required, you must develop your own plan of action. The skilled trades typically do a three-year cycle. You can develop your own professional development plan that will occur in a three-year cycle, as well.

Some best practices for you to consider are:

Self-Care

- Set time in your morning for quiet time so that you can gather your thoughts and plan your day.
- Set time in each day for at least 15-30 minutes of workout.
- Join an association (industry, ethnicity, degree-related, title-related).
- Regularly attend networking events (once a quarter, twice a year, etc.).
- Read at least four books a year (include something motivational, industry-specific).
- Subscribe to services that provide you with weekly updates that support your job.

Performance:

- Show up to everything 15 minutes early.
- Do the right thing all the times.
- Be present in every meeting and conversation (undivided attention).
- Show up prepared for the moment.
- Leave all personal issues at the door.
- If you are invited to a meeting, don't be afraid to ask about the agenda/topic:
    - Be prepared. Study the topic, know what points you need to address and come prepared with solutions.
    - If you are the junior person in the room (and you may not

be in the seat of authority to ask questions), follow up with your manager and circle back to any solutions you may have.

    o   Always know your action items and your deadlines.

- Admit when you have made a mistake.
- Celebrate your successes.

Relationships

- Have at least one mentor. If you are juggling multiple careers, you might want to consider more than one mentor.
- Have a few friends that are operating in the space you are striving for. Some of these may become informal mentors.
- Build rapport with colleagues that are healthy. Not all colleagues are meant to be friends.
- If you are married, make sure you and your spouse have great communication and shared vision. Support each other.

You must develop your brand reputation. Own *you*. Master what you do. Let dependability be your badge. Do not overextend yourself. Be confident in saying, "I don't know." If you develop your self-image as I am outlining and suggesting, you will have an enhanced life. Promotions may come. You will become more assertive and chart a winning course for your life. So, keep your image always in front of you and you will *win*!

Optimistic While Nailing (OWN) Your Image

Reflections

1. Now that you have finished this chapter, take five minutes to reflect on what you have read and the questions you have

answered. Write two statements to describe how you might apply
this information to your life.

1. ____

   ____

2. ____

   ____

2. What are three actionable items that you can put in place today
to improve your image?

1. ____

2. ____

3. ____

Dr. Crystal Cooper

*"Grace opens doors toward meaningful
and memorable relationships."*

It IS all about YOU-M.O.D.E.L-G.R.A.C.E.

Imagine changing the narrative of it *not being about you* to *it is about you*. As a leader, we are oftentimes influenced by trying to fit into the many characteristics of thought leaders, innovators and authors. They tell us how to be leaders regarding relationships, attitude and the execution of a mission. As novice and veteran leaders, it is critical that we build a positive bridge between ourselves and those we lead. The hope is that this bridge will not only model care and understanding, but that it would also urge those who follow us to surpass personal and professional goals.

The premise of this chapter is to help you gain some leadership tidbits that will help you delve *within* to become the leader who others will connect and engage with on a higher level. The hope also is that it will ultimately make you the kind of leader that the world will be attracted to, enough to advance an organization's vision and goals, no matter what industry you are in.

Growing up as an only child, I learned leadership at a young age. Often being named "bossy" by my teachers and peers, I utilized the title to scaffold myself as a leader from elementary school until now. I led many clubs in college and performed in various talent entities, while persevering through four colleges to gain my doctorate and become a school principal.

This century has evolved to make leadership models visual, transparent and quickly accessible. Among social media tweets and posts, we now see the act of leadership in various ways. Though not always one to emulate, we have seen those in leadership show themselves to the world as either positive or negative influencers. What it tells us is that leadership *is* a heavy influencer and change agent. It can cause you to change, execute a vision, and make the critical leadership moves needed to fulfill a mission in our personal and professional lives.

I have designed some tidbits to consider when making the leap to leadership, transformation and sustainment. I not only reflected on my own leadership with 22 years in education, but I also gathered feedback from my employees over the years, who added great value to this context.

A leader must always M.O.D.E.L. G.R.A.C.E.

Model positivity and leadership in every interaction.

Own the vision and mission.

Develop employees through professional learning experiences.

Empathize with all stakeholders and their personal journeys.

Lead by example.

Give genuine feedback and support.

Respect them, and they will respect you.

Always reflect on who you are in your role, and recalibrate.

Correct lovingly.

Empower others to be leaders.

Model Positivity and Leadership in Every Interaction

A leader is one who understands the power of a positive work environment. When considering every decision made, they do so by asking, "What impact will this have on the climate and the positive work environment? Is this change necessary now, or is it possible to forego this change in order to maintain an environment where employees can thrive?"

I have had to make many decisions as a principal. I have had to be decisive and laser-focused with regard to how my decisions would affect each teacher's ability to feel supported and cared for throughout the decision-making process. Your positive insight must be felt, heard and consistent. Your facial expressions and body language, when employees ask questions, is key. When someone asks a question, do you show frustration? Or do you model openness in your stance? These questions are key in creating positive moments as a leader. There is power in conversation; therefore, you must have a listening ear and a positive mindset when correcting, reprimanding or supporting. Every interaction matters and it speaks to your overall leadership quality. Be mindful of every moment when you are with others. You are a walking commercial.

Own the Vision and Mission

A vision is a goal for the future. It's what your organization ascribes to be and reaches toward for the future. A mission is the right now. What is the company doing right now? What does that company stand for? We may have all heard these questions, but have we memorized our company's mission and vision so that it becomes a living, breathing environment? If anyone knows the vision and mission of the company, it should be the leaders. When you know the mission and vision, it transcends in every decision you make. Your staff will know and understand why you make the decisions you do. You will be able to refer to the annual goals through the vision and mission when needed. Organically, it becomes a natural part of your "why," and it builds more allegiance to building an organization of followers. Memorize it, embed it and execute it into all moves you make.

Develop Them Through Professional Learning Experiences

Do *you* value learning? If leading by example is something you believe in, it must start with you. Read leadership books, stay connected with other leadership experts and be present with your staff through professional learning experiences. If they view you as a lifetime learner, they will be more apt to desire more learning. It will exude in all you do. Your excitement for learning will naturally make your people seek more knowledge. Know the leading industry leaders in your field and task yourself with creating a system where you are constantly staying fully engrossed in the latest research-based information. This will build your credibility in the field. If people see you as a learner, they will believe in you and follow you because you are knowledgeable. Be knowledgeable and act knowledgeable.

Empathize with Others and Their Personal Journeys

Leadership is a heart matter. It involves knowing your people and allowing them to feel your presence in their lives. Everyone has a personal journey where they embark on various challenges that may bleed into the workplace. Keep a journal with the name of each employee you lead. When something happens in their life, jot it down and, most importantly, follow up. Do you know their strengths, their favorites and their family life? With the trials of life, it is hard to come to work and focus. When their leader understands that, it models compassion, flexibility and trust, which are three things that all leaders must possess.

Reflect on Webster's definition of empathy: *"the action of understanding, being aware of, being sensitive to, and vicariously experiencing the feelings, thoughts, and experience of another of either the past or present without having the feelings, thoughts, and experience fully communicated in an objectively explicit manner; also: the capacity for this."* Consider your staff all the time and create a system to let them know you are fully engaged.

Lead by Example

In his book, *Attitude 101*, John Maxwell says, "People always project on the outside how they feel on the inside" (Maxwell, 2003). Therefore, we must always reflect on our own humanity and our attitude. Do you show transparency, forgiveness and integrity in all you do? The act of modeling integrity will lead others to trust you. It's fine at times to offer a small peek into your personal life, your challenges and your weaknesses. I have shown interest in others and taken the time to follow up with them. People feel important if they know you care. I have several opportunities to model servant leadership by how I ask questions, use eye contact and focus in conversations. This was not always easy for me. I have had to work on it because my principal life is vast, fast-paced and unpredictable. Nevertheless, I find it essential to model leadership in every interaction with my community, students, parents and staff.

We also make mistakes as leaders. So, we need to learn how to apologize, take constructive criticism and empathize with others. If we do not, we will not gain committed followers. People want to hear that you get them and that you are not above reproach. Your failures show them that you have truly sat in their shoes (walk in their shoes?) and that you understand the ebb and flow of life.

Finally, when crisis hits your office, how do you handle it? Catastrophizing everything causes others to feel unsafe and that you can't be trusted. I have had several emergencies ensue at my school. Through all of these challenges, I was conscious of my face, my mannerisms and my comments. You must model positivity, calmness and knowledge at all times because they look to you for guidance. Be the example of grace, leadership and expertise. They are watching your leadership moves. Move consciously.

Ask yourself, "What would be on my leadership banner if I were to fly it for all to see? What would others say about me if they were to tell someone else what kind of leader I am?"

Give Genuine Feedback and Support

Whenever I reflect on my leadership practices, I think of the largest mistake I made, which came from a lack of follow-through. As a principal, we are supposed to conduct frequent classroom walkthroughs. I realized that I was not observing and following up with timely feedback for my staff. Because I didn't want to create an environment where I micromanaged everyone and everything, I did not observe as frequently. I was working, but I was only "dropping in" classrooms to do what I call, "pity pat" coaching. I was not truly observing, sitting and listening, or checking in with students to see if they were truly learning. Therefore, I had no context of what was truly happening in the classroom. I had an assumption, but no facts. I was leading under the misconception that all was okay.

This year, with a new administrative staff of assistant principals, we committed to the popular directive of, "Inspect what you expect." Therefore, more collaborative conversations ensued with staff. They needed feedback to confirm, reinforce or redirect them toward school goals. Sit with your teams in planning meetings. Don't always be the director; be the participant. Work with them and learn with them. You must be the leader of genuine feedback whose goal is to transform and uplift to excellence.

Respect Them, and They Will Respect You

I had never heard this said so profoundly, but one of my staff members relayed this important message about model leadership to me. When I consider the value of respect, I think of how powerful this statement is. Do we think before we speak, and just ignore their feelings because it is their job? One time, a former leader said to me, "They are supposed to do it. It's their job." I said, "Yes, it is. But if we believe this in all we do, and interact with this mindset regarding our teams, we are going to position ourselves for a downhill turn. Respect them, show it and live it. They will, in turn, respect you. Ask their opinion and gather their input. Let them know that you trust them."

Say it: "I trust you." These three words are needed to build a high-functioning work environment. When they fail, which some will, hold them up, re-train them, and allow them to recalibrate. Model respect by smiling, speaking to them in passing and holding short regular conversations that allow you to connect and engage. Honor them for their birthday. Share in life events, whether positive or negative. Most of all, have a sense of humor.

One of my most popular leadership moves is my personal letter writing ritual that I have conducted for the eighth year as principal. The night before the first day of school, I write a personal handwritten note to *all* of my staff members. It takes me an entire day, but it is worth it. From the administrators, office staff and teachers, to custodians and cafeteria workers, it is one of the most positive leader moves that has made a difference in my school climate. People want to feel like they belong. They want to feel like they are significant. Do not just email them to offer a compliment. Call them and give them a handwritten note to recognize them often. Take a list of your staff and highlight those you have given a letter to already. Review this list daily. The time spent investing in this practice will offer major dividends in the end.

Always Reflect on Who You Are and How Your Strengths Affect Your Abilities

When we are leaders, we have to slow down to observe ourselves, listen to others' point of view, and recalibrate. When we take the time to learn our own strengths and weaknesses, coupled with the willingness to gather feedback, we have modeled a high level of leadership. We all have natural talents. When we focus on those, we have more room for our growth to exist (Rath, 2007).

"So, a revision to the "You-can-be-anything-you-want-to-be" maxim might be more accurate: You *cannot* be anything you want to be. But you *can* be a lot more of who you already are" (Rath, pg. 9., 2007).

In 2007, I was gifted the book, *Strengthsfinder®*, by Tom Rath. This book transformed my leadership and personal journey. This book was introduced to me when I participated in a leadership cohort for aspiring principals. I have since introduced it to many associates, staff members and friends. What this book teaches readers is that we must work to develop our strengths, which will, in turn, be more important than our role, title or even our pay (Rath, 2007). With 10 million people being surveyed on this specific topic, they found that approximately seven million people lacked the ability to focus on what they did best. I learned that when you are not in your strengths zone, you are six times less likely to be engaged on your job.

When you are not able to use your strengths at work, chances are that you:

- Dislike going to work

- Have more negative interactions than positive ones

- Treat customers inappropriately

- Achieve less on a daily basis

    - Have fewer positive and creative moments

We all will change over time; however, we all have core personality traits that do not change much over time, as do our passions and interests (Rath, 2007). Having a strengths-based approach has a positive alignment with our wellness, relationships, confidence, direction and kindness toward others.

Correct Lovingly

As a leader, I have made mistakes. There were times when I was called into the principal's office "to be corrected." Due to others modeling this in positive and negative ways over the years, I have been able to decide how I wanted to be treated. I have always thought of how to handle these difficult conversations. When considering feedback from my staff from a recent survey, coupled with interviews, they value my ability to hold conversations with them that are always positive in nature. I also model patience with correction.

Sometimes, people need time to fix their inappropriate actions. When applicable, observe, take notes and do not always feel the need to "pounce" on every move they make. Once you feel that enough has occurred, discuss some of the improvements needed and set a plan for the improvement process. This will speak volumes to your constituents of how you handle and approach correction.

Consider where you speak with your employees. Can you meet with them in their space or environment? If not, consider a neutral environment. I will speak with individuals in my office for positive conversations and planning, and their classrooms or space for directive or feedback.

Finally, for serious consequences, we will meet in a more formal space, such as the conference room. These spaces strategically model the level of intensity of the situation and speak to care and compassion for their well-being. Smile, when needed. Position yourself across from them and be confidential. One way to ruin your credibility as a leader is to spread the conversation with others. If your conversation requires whispering, close the door. Whispering carries and sends a negative message. Value the conversation, and model integrity and respect at all times.

Empower Others to be Leaders

My goal has always been to make a list of those I have helped grow, promote or lead. I did not know the impact I had on so many in my 22 years of education. Whether in my midst for a long amount of time or not, I have taken the liberty to help others move forward in their careers. I was always appreciative of those who saw something in me and desired to push me. That push is exactly what your employees need to feel. They need to feel like they belong and that they are significant.

I have created a local leadership academy at my school and created opportunities for others to lead. Just by saying, "I see more for you," or "I see leadership in you," can move others to become more aligned with their purpose, which makes them work harder. This will separate them from the naysayers and help them work toward their next best thing. The downfall to this is that you lose great people and you are always hiring, building and replacing. However, it is still a win-win for you. When that person is asked, "Where did you work?" he or she will be a walking commercial for you. You will be known as the leader who promotes and builds. More will view you as the bridge to encouragement. They will believe in themselves and desire more opportunities. In my tenure, I have observed more than 50 individuals get promoted or improved with my prodding and pushing. It is a joy to watch others succeed.

I haven't always got it right. Know that my presence in the leadership arena came with tears, major disappointments and fears. However, I have always been built with a high level of faith, perseverance and belief in my purpose. I have read, researched, set goals and remained focused on what I desired in my career. I have also modeled leadership in whom I hired. Be intrinsically motivated to make those around you feel valued and important continuously.

As you embark on your leadership journey for the first time, or the 100th time, always look at yourself in the mirror. It is *always* about *you*. You can always turn the page and make a new *you*. Be transparent and let your team know your strengths, weaknesses, personal journey and human side. Execute the organization's mission with fidelity. Follow a process that allows you to create continuous growth opportunities to build a viable leadership environment.

I encourage you to lead ambitiously, continuously learning about yourself and those you lead. I hope it has encouraged you to understand your worth, value and influence in the area of leadership. May you always model grace!

Questions:

1. What ways do you proactively lead with grace and understanding as a leader?

2. If given a chance to improve your leadership practices tomorrow, what area of M.O.D.E.L.G.R.A.C.E. could you implement?

Dr. Melissa A. Brunson

I am a strong, confident and caring woman, with a healthy perspective about life, and all that it has to offer.   I welcome the opportunity to face challenges, learn from my mistakes, and experience positive changes so that I can be my best self. I don't allow people or obstacles to stunt my growth.

Leadership that Brings All Onboard

During a segment of my teaching years, I remember looking forward to the first month of summer break with the anticipation of relaxing and rejuvenating, putting a sacred distance between work and my personal life. I spent the second month feeling enthusiastic about reinforcing my skills and pedagogical knowledge. I participated in workshops, attended conferences, and re-engaged with my colleagues in preparation for the upcoming school year. As the summer break days drew closer to pre-service, my excitement waned, just thinking about what my leaders were planning for the new school year. I wondered what the new school's "golden rules" and mission that I had to get accustomed to, without question, interruption, or input from my colleagues and I. Although teaching was something I loved and was highly passionate about, I often felt overlooked and underappreciated by school leadership because I had no say in the making of school decisions. My colleagues and I would receive little to no recognition for our work, resulting in low morale, reduced efficiency, and high staff turnover.

Student achievement and teacher effectiveness and retention are affected hallmarks for a school. Research has shown that student achievement will happen in positive school climates where staff feel valued, respected, and cared for. By creating opportunities for staff to be involved in the development of the school-wide vision, decisions, and school improvement planning a positive school culture is created and cultivated. The experiences I had under autocratic leadership inspired me to further my educational leadership talent, develop the skills to be a democratic leader, and join the ranks of other successful administrators who wanted to affect change. During my time as a school-based leader, I employed a more democratic, collaborative leadership style, that yielded positive results. It is my greatest hope that current and future leaders who read this chapter recognize the enormous impact they have to the success of an organization and will understand what it means to get "All Onboard."

As a distinguished educational leader, my purpose is to enrich the lives of children with an excellent education. My main goal is to maintain and grow rigorous, safe learning environments that provide students with the opportunity to cultivate habits of the mind and skills that are necessary to pursue their dreams and goals beyond high school.

In order to sustain this effort, I have worked collaboratively with our exceptional educational and community leaders as a special education teacher, and as a school-based and central office leader for more than 22 years. As an extension of my doctoral work, I collaborated with others to lay the groundwork for elementary principals to receive ongoing technology leadership professional development in one of the largest school districts in the country. Additionally, I have taken steps to empower potential teacher leaders to serve as mentors and/or consider leadership positions where their skills could be best utilized.

In my role as principal developer, I have supported and built the instructional leadership capacity of aspiring administrators, assistant principals on track to becoming principals, who have all progressed to becoming instructional leaders in their respective schools. I led roundtable and panel discussions at educational conferences and meetings, including, but not limited to, The International Conference on Urban Education, Young Education D.C. Professionals, and The American Enterprise Institute, which is focused on principal leadership in the 21st century.

In these roles, I was able to provide strategic direction for teaching and learning. By connecting sound instructional administrative leadership, and teaching practices to unique academic programs and wraparound services, I worked tirelessly to produce measurable gains in student achievement outcomes, attendance, graduation and post-secondary supports. My background and personal experiences have paved the way for my successful educational leadership career.

Cultivating an All Onboard Vision

When I served as a school principal, I was intentional about creating a vision – one that is shared by all. Inherent in my school's vision statement, "The school community is dedicated to ensuring success for every student in an inclusive and caring environment," are my core beliefs about how education should be applied on a school-based level. To ensure that all students were making progress, we, the teachers and administrators, engaged in daily, weekly and quarterly dialogue that included analyzing quantitative and qualitative achievement data, planning for instruction, and monitoring student progress. Part of my leadership role was to make sure the vision was clear and to ensure that our actions aligned with our core values.

Are employees clear about the vision of your organization? Do they understand and do they apply the core values undergirding this important work? Many companies have adopted the Disney structure of "onboarding". This is to ensure that employees truly understand the mission and vision of an organization, and that they can apply them to their job duties. Onboarding happens early on in the hiring process, which allows employees to consider if they truly want to work for a particular company. I have had the opportunity to facilitate onboarding within my school district, and I found it to be a valuable experience for employees entering our organization.

As employees engage in the hustle and bustle of work, serving and interacting with clients, adjusting to changes within the organization, and managing their personal lives, employees tend to lose focus of the vision. I have witnessed this over and over again as a leader. It's important to revisit the reason why we are here (visioning) through artifacts, quotes and pictures, which can be seen and even heard throughout the organization. Messaging through newsletters, social media, memorandums and other forms of communication should have imprints of this level of communication. Once a week, I put out a Monday Message to my staff with reminders of upcoming events and messages that remind us of the school's vision. Here is an example of an excerpt I included in a Monday Message:

Final Message...As you know, Equity in the Classroom is one of
the focal points for this school year. As XX and I conduct informal
walk-throughs, we will be providing you with reflective feedback as you
are implementing equitable practices that will provide the assurance

When I published these weekly messages, staff were reminded of the school's vision in connection with our established expectations.

All Onboard Decision-Making

Top-down decision-making is one of the least productive leadership practices. I read somewhere about an 80/20 rule, where 80% of a leader's decisions should be shared, and 20% should be made solo, especially if you are seeking a high level of commitment from employees. Besides, your employees are the ones who are most responsible for providing direct service to the client. In my profession, it would be teachers serving students.

Top-down, or authoritative decision-making, is great for compliance. But commitment by employees tends to be low because they are just doing what the boss tells them to do, mainly out of fear. Similar to how students feel when they are forced to follow classroom rules they didn't create, you may experience rebellion and a lack of commitment and support from employees toward the effort. It is important that employees have some level of ownership; otherwise, the plan is doomed to fail and morale is affected.

One example of shared leadership in the field of education is the process that is used to develop the school's improvement plan. It is critical to pull a representative sample of stakeholders - teachers, support staff and parents – whose responsibility was to work collaboratively to develop the plan. The school improvement plan requires a deep analysis of the school's academic data and other measures taken through surveys that captivate student, staff and parent voices. As a part of the analysis process, we ask, "Why?" This should be asked several times to determine a root cause. Additional inquiries can be made regarding what worked, what didn't work, what we would like to keep, and what needs to be refined are a significant part of the process that help teams take a deep dive into the data.

The group of stakeholders use their collective voice to engage in the analysis of the data and work together to create a strategic plan. This includes the school's and the district's missions, core values, strategic direction, instructional focus goals, action plans, and the process for monitoring the attainment of this goal. The role of the principal is to serve as a facilitator, ensuring that the process is fair and equitable, and that the plan is in alignment with the school and the school district's direction. Of course, this can be applied to any leader who is responsible for facilitating the development of a strategic plan.

The individuals involved in developing the plan become cheerleaders for its implementation. Once the plan is presented, with the understanding that representative members of the staff were involved in its creation, others will follow suit. Knowing that a collective voice participated in creating the plan, the practitioners are highly likely to implement it with fidelity. Their commitment level becomes stronger when the plan is monitored, results are reported, and there are opportunities to celebrate positive results. If modifications to the plan are required, employees typically understand, as long as they remain involved in the decision-making process.

During my tenure as a school principal, I understood the obstacles that I faced. Too many things get in the way of providing excellent leadership, such as personnel issues, district mandates and compliance. I found myself spending less time on instruction, such as observing teaching and learning, and professional development planning and implementation, than I would have liked. By sharing ways in which I facilitated a shared vision, I engaged employees with shared decision-making as it related to school improvement planning. Those I supervised remained connected to this important work. I have experienced success and made a difference in the lives of students.

Questions:

1. What aspects of your personal life story and experiences influence who you are as a leader?
2. How do your core values define who you are as a leader? How do your personal beliefs and attitudes align with what is valued by your organization?
3. What techniques or strategies do you have in place that inspire a high level of commitment from your employees?
4. What strategies do you have in place to ensure that your vision is alive and well in your organization?
5. How do your employees contribute to the decision-making in your organization?
6. How well are you employing strategic planning processes to ensure continuous improvement in your organization?

It is essential that all organizations create vision and mission statements and strategic action plans for continuous improvement. Those statements and plans must be aligned with the overall mission and core values of the organization at all times and must be revisited often. Successful implementation of these processes are contingent upon the consistency of the following practices:

- Collaborating with stakeholder groups to develop and monitor organization-wide goals.

- Ensuring that ongoing quality professional development is provided to all professionals.

- Analyzing data to ensure the goals are met.

In order for organizations to achieve excellent results, its members must know the vision, so it can be observed in their everyday walk and talk. When leaders don't implement processes to establish and embrace a shared vision, individuals become disconnected, disenchanted, and feel disrespected; some will leave the organization. Our job as leaders is to ensure everyone stays on track to meet the desired goals of the organization.

Dr Arthur Williams

*I must pursue my destiny because someone's life depends
on me being extraordinary in all areas of my life.*

Are You Up on Your Leadership Game?

Leadership is like a game; one must learn how to maintain momentum while in pursuit of their goals of winning the game. Whether one is a leader in their home, church or community, or they hold a formal leadership position in an organization, one thing is for sure: challenges will come! Opposition will come. Leaders must be strategic in how they face adaptive challenges. Too often, bold, passionate leaders become discouraged on their leadership journey because of the bruising, scolding, mistakes, setbacks and disappointments that occur while leading others. There is a mindset that will help leaders to maintain traction and progress. I call it the UP Typology. *Up* is a mindset. If leaders are going to be effective, they must Wake *Up*, Get *Up*, Stay *Up*, and Tune *Up*, no matter the opposition.

Wake Up

Overcoming the Status Quo

"Congratulations, Mr. Williams! You were the interview panel's top choice. We are pleased to recommend your appointment to the new leadership position."

This is the dream of everyone who strives to secure a leadership position in an organization. That phrase, "Congratulations!" is like music to one's ears. The hard work finally paid off. The risk of leaving one city in search of an opportunity in another city was worth it! Or was it?

You know that moment when you have completed what you thought was your entry work and unpacked the culture of the new organization. You have toured the building, met key influencers, reviewed the data and conducted a community scan. You identified key constituents and you're clear of the metrics that must be met at all levels of the organization. You have even identified potential adaptive challenges and barriers. Yes, that moment is here. You knew that moment would come. You did not know when or how, but it has arrived!

What is that moment, you ask? It's the moment when the euphoria from obtaining that dream leadership position abruptly gives way to the reality of leading a new organization through a change process. Suddenly, the honeymoon is over! It is time for change and new initiatives. This includes work schedules, staff changes, new policies and practices, more bureaucratic restructures, and responding to constituents' desires for improved results. In the midst of all of this change, employees revert back to "doing things like they had always been done." They fall back on the status quo when no one is looking. The status quo is familiar and whether good or bad, it is comfortable. In order to maintain organizational momentum, leaders must be willing to "wake up" and challenge the status quo.

It has been my experience that, when leading an organization through a change process, people fall into one of the following types.

- *Yes, I will go.*

- *Yes, I may go!*

- *No, it doesn't make sense!*

- *No, I am not going!*

I must admit that when I came into contact with the latter group, I assumed people were resistant and not committed to the mission. At times, sadly, I felt like the individuals were just buying time. In actuality, those individuals had experience and wisdom. It was not until I learned that all change or innovation must start with the leader understanding the mindsets of the people. After assessing the mindset of the individuals, you are leading, then and only then can you begin to challenge the status quo.

When you "wake up" and challenge the status quo, leaders should consider the following: First, make your vision personable and simple so that everyone can share in the vision. Leaders need not overwhelm members in an organization with vague jargon and catchy phrases. However, time should be devoted to communicating the vision in ways that are relatable, and in a way that causes an emotional reaction and confronts the level of uncertainty head on.

Secondly, leverage relationships with influencers. Influencers are people who may not necessarily hold formal authority, but they are valued and respected by members of the organization. You know these people. They are the ones who, when they speak, people listen and act. Thirdly, overcoming the status quo will compel leaders to deal with the level of uncertainty that may exist in an organizational culture. Simply put, leaders need to show members of the organization successful models or practices that have helped other organizations become successful.

Additionally, leaders must foster collaboration. In their book, *The Leadership Challenge*, Kouzes and Posner state, "You can't do it alone is the mantra of exemplary leaders—and for good reason. You can't make extraordinary things happen by yourself. It's a collaboration that enables corporations, communities and even virtual classrooms to function effectively." This happens by building relationships and creating an atmosphere of trust. Leaders must paint a picture of the future and make it clear how each person will benefit the organization. Effective leaders must be willing to wake up the organization or community they lead by challenging the status quo head on so momentum can be maintained. *So, wake up!*

Questions to Ponder

1. How are you building trust with others?

2. Who are the key influencers in your organization and how can you leverage your relationship to create a shared vision?

3. What is the status quo culture that needs to be tackled?

Get Up

Overcoming Fear

Peter Guber, owner and co-executive chairman of the Golden State Warriors stated, "Fear can paralyze or catalyze an organization. Leaders' willingness to embrace fear dictates how successful they and their enterprise may be. Leaders must tell a story that makes fear an ally, not an adversary, ultimately conveying the message that fear — F.E.A.R. — is "false evidence appearing real" (Guber, 2011).

Every leader has to deal with the fear factor of leadership. To be accountable for everything is daunting, to say the least. I recall a time when I accepted a job in a new city. It was a great promotion and a position that I always wanted. I confronted the fear that prevented me from stepping out of my comfort zone prior to this opportunity in the past. So, I was excited that I got past my fear and pursued this new opportunity. I was so proud of myself until I got into the flow of the work. I quickly realized that this new city and new organization had a deep culture and outsiders were not welcomed. No matter how nice I tried to be or how I attempted to collaborate with others, it just seemed like I faced one obstacle after the next. In one instance, three of my colleagues, who were supervisors like me, would routinely not share information that impacted all the units we were supervising. I remember seeing black ribbons outside of certain people's doors and wondered what that was about. I asked Mr. Grooms, a veteran employee and someone I supervised, for honest feedback about what I could do to make better connections with people.

"Leave," Mr. Grooms said. "People believe you were brought in to get rid of everyone, especially us veteran folk. There were many days when I did not want to go to work and when I pulled up to the office, I would have knots in my stomach."

Then, it dawned on me: just as I was experiencing fear, many in the organization that I was leading were extremely fearful. So, we all became victims to F.E.A.R— "false evidence appearing real." It took time to build trust, but I learned that fear can play out in many ways, and perception has a lot to do with it.

I was living both the *noun* of fear, which is *an unpleasant emotion caused by the belief that someone or something is dangerous, likely to cause pain, or a threat,* as well as the *verb* of fear, which means *to be afraid of (someone or something) as likely to be dangerous, painful, or threatening.*

In the subsequent weeks and days, I had to lead my unit in the midst of fear. Fear is a strong emotion. Leaders, at some point on their leadership journey, will have to "get up," face their fears and keep the momentum going.

Effective leaders must attend to the present reality, which requires leaders to meet people where they are. First, allow forums for people to be open and honest. People want to be heard, so it is incumbent for leaders to listen intently. "The leader must look for quick wins. Examine where the energy is in the organization and give the individuals you serve the thing they perceive will improve their efficiency and productivity.

I recently learned of a protocol called "feedback on feedback." Basically, you share with employees what they have requested, and you show them what you have done in response to the request. This strategy allows people to be truly heard and they know you have acted on it. In the classic work by Kouzes and Posner, *The Leadership Challenge*, the authors suggest that connecting to what's meaningful to others involves understanding.

"What truly pulls people forward, especially in more challenging and volatile times, is the exciting possibility that what they are doing can make a profound difference in the lives of their families, friends, colleagues, customers and communities. They want to know what they do matters" (Kouzes and Posner, 2017).

Once I understood this, I reminded people of our common purpose: helping meet the organizational targets and provide outstanding service to our partners. Secondly, leaders must help those in the organization acknowledge their own fears during a transition or a turbulent time. Whether a financial crisis or tragedy, leaders must demonstrate compassion. Leaders must listen to the concerns of others. I spent countless hours showing that I cared. I wrote notes and letters to individuals, thanking them for their efforts. I would ask, "How are you doing today?" I looked for ways to alleviate staff from some organizational tasks that could be done at a later date.

Thirdly, staying the course is the ultimate challenge for any leader. Don't lose momentum. Leaders must rely on their training and ability to connect with others and forge ahead. Leaders must continue to offer hope and keep moving toward the goals. Leaders cannot allow momentary setbacks to immobilize their team. Leaders must work with constituents and march forward! *Get up!*

Questions to Ponder

1. How do you deal with fear?

2. In what ways do you connect with others?

3. How can you listen deeply to others and act on what you hear in tangible ways?

Stay Up

Overcoming the Complacency Barrier

"Dr. Williams, can I meet with you to discuss our team's progress?"

"Yes! Let's meet at 1 p.m."

I was hoping to hear how a team leader was leading her team through the new program that we had been implementing for the past two years. I had reviewed data recently and noted some progress.

However, when Ms. Conner marched into my office, she said, "We need to do something. I know we can implement this program better."

"What do you think is the problem?" I asked.

"Complacency."

Complacency can creep up on any leader, if one fails to pay attention. Jim Collins said it best in the book, *From Good to Great*, "Good is the enemy of great." We have all experienced it from time to time. Sometimes, the signs are apparent when it appears that teams are doing just enough to get by or leaders are setting easy, attainable targets. You may have seen it written in vision statements, such as, "We expect 80 percent of ________________." Why not 100 percent? Complacency is a huge barrier to maintaining organizational momentum.

In the book, *Leading Change* by John Kotter, he suggests that leaders must understand the difference between management and leadership. A management approach may settle on controlling and problem solving. This involves monitoring results, identifying deviation from the plan, and then planning and organizing to solve the complacency problem. A leadership approach would tackle the complacency issues by motivating and inspiring others. This involves energizing people to overcome major political, bureaucratic and resource barriers to change by satisfying basic, but often unfulfilled, human needs.

One may argue that both approaches are needed or important, but during times of stagnation, leaders must watch out for complacency. In my experience, complacency is a silent drain that can derail an organization. So, how do you overcome the complacency syndrome? You must "*stay up!*" Les Robinson offers a framework that is worthy of consideration. It goes like this:

If there's positive buzz,
And we offer hope,
And a sticky solution,
And expanded comfort zones,
And the right inviter (invitation)
Then people will do things they have never done before and sustain those changes.

When I reflect on my leadership journey, I have been there—complacent. I allowed myself to settle into mundane routines. Regrettably, I missed opportunities to stay engaged and connected to the work. In her leadership blog post entitled, *Surviving Leadership*, leadership expert Mary Faulkner suggests that "an organization is a shadow of the leader." Faulkner elaborates on this point by stating:

"The leader of an organization casts a shadow that influences the group culture. This shadow may be weak or powerful, but it always exists. Whole organizations often take on aspects of the personality of a strong leader (think Apple, Microsoft, Southwest, Virgin, etc.) It's not so much that leaders force their style and values on others, but that employees tend to look upwards for clues as to what is important, how to get ahead in the organization, and how to fit in. This is the power of the shadow in action - the power to shape and influence the character of an organization" (Faulkner, 2013).

So, if the organization you lead has become stagnant, look inside yourself and ask the hard questions. What are you casting? Have you, as a leader, become complacent in your thoughts, words, actions or deeds? Reflect on that, then make a conscience decision to *"stay up!"*

Tune Up

Rediscover Your Passion

Leaders seeking to overcome the complacency barrier should consider what I call a "tune up." First, leaders must rediscover their passion. Start by making a list of three to five things that excite you about your work. Place that list somewhere you can refer back to it. On my desk and under my computer, I have three simple sentences that remind me of my purpose. I refer to it often when I feel unmotivated. Secondly, selfishly take time to invest in your own skill set, which will help you to lead at a higher level. Share your learning and excitement with others. This can become contagious. You will create an amazing environment when leaders begin to share with each other. Thirdly, celebrate small accomplishments, whether they are personal or within the organization.

Make the celebration a regular part of the organizational culture. Look for testimonials and evidence that progress is being made. Being the change, you wish to see requires a "tune up" to ensure that momentum is maintained!

Questions to Ponder

1. What excites you about your work?

2. What learning have you engaged in to support your excitement?

3. How do you celebrate personal accomplishments and those of others?

Lisa Coker

__The steps of the righteous are ordered by the Lord.__ When I look back over my life, I can see where He has ordered my steps from the beginning! I am a product of teenage parents (Mom and Dad married at age 15 and 18, respectively), and divorced by the time I was five years old. I was raised, for the most part, by my mom, as a single parent. Statistically speaking, a young black child from a broken home is not expected to fare as well as children from two-parent homes. So, based on the world's expectations, I should have been one of those statistics. My answer to that statistic is "But…God." "For I know the plans I have for you," declares the LORD, "plans to prosper you and not to harm you, plans to give you hope and a future" (Jeremiah 29:11, NIV).

Open Letter to Younger Self

In this chapter, I write my *younger* self a letter of lessons learned, affirmations and what I know for sure. I believe this letter honors the experience and knowledge I have gained, thus far, in my journey to discovering my purpose. I hope it will *encourage* you to become deliberate about the pursuit of your gifts and to use them in service to others.

Dear Lil Lisa,

Seek and Operate in God's Purpose for Your Life

The first thing I want you to know is that you must seek the Lord's will for your life's purpose. Remember to be a God-fearing woman—a woman of your word, a woman with integrity, and a woman who walks in love. Now, that is a tall order; so you, Lil Lisa, will want to start *early* in honing these skills. This will require that you follow God's teachings: learn to treat others as you would have them treat you (The Golden Rule); do the right thing even when others are not looking (integrity); and strive to *do* and to *be* the "very best" you can *be*. Know that God will help you and He will work in your life to get His will accomplished.

Search your heart, and once you know you have given it your all, well—that's all that's required of you (but when your best is not good enough, it's "okay"…the earth will still keep spinning and the sun will still shine). Oh yes, take advantage of the opportunities that come your way! You never know where those opportunities will lead you. Pursue and do well with small opportunities because they will lead to bigger and greater opportunities. Education is important to a degree. Your education helps you to get into the room. But, your work ethic, integrity and determination help get you a seat at the table.

Mistakes Happen, Might as Well Use Them

The second thing I want you to know is that you have permission to make mistakes. In fact, the process of growth, maturity *and* success depends heavily on you "making mistakes" and quickly learning from them! Note: The key to making mistakes is *learning*—I repeat, *learning* from them – fail fast and fix forward are two of my favorite entrepreneurial quotes. While some mistakes are necessary, others are avoidable. This means that you don't have to *personally* make every mistake; you can rely on other's mistakes and lessons learned to inform your decisions. Simply put, be willing to learn from others!

The key to learning from others is to *listen*—not only with your ears, but with your heart. You do not have to reinvent the wheel. Follow the road map laid out by those who have gone before you and paved the way. You can always *make adjustments* to suit your own situation. Understand that wisdom *and* growth can come from positive and negative outcomes. I know you are going to be afraid with every new endeavor, but take the leap, stay the course and trust the process.

Share Your Life's Journey with the Next Generation

The third and final thing I want you to know is to *enjoy life's journey (the ups and the downs)*. You will have to *cut yourself some slack*—learn what is important and what can wait. Take time out for yourself and do some of what brings *you* joy. Each step you take is all a part of becoming *you*.

Oh, yes! And should you get married and have children (trust me, *you will*) make certain you take time to instill in them these same principles. Children truly are the future. Oh, *cut them some slack, too*. You weren't perfect; you made mistakes and they will also.

Part of enjoying the journey is to understand what it means to take time to smell the roses. Simply put, don't discount the seemingly small things because they will truly become the *big* things in a life well lived.

Now go and *give it your all and do all to the glory of God.*

God loves and values you and so do I!

Signed,

Me

Positive Affirmations:

We have to believe God values us and speak "life" over our lives (and that of our children/family). I know that there is life and death in the power of our tongues and those who love it will eat its fruits (Proverbs 18:21), so choose to speak life over yourself, your family and your situation. I constantly remind myself that *I am more than enough, I can do all things through Christ who strengthens me, knock and the door will be opened to me; seek and I will find,* etc. I really speak these affirmations over my life, and I have seen the difference in what happens as a result. In high school, I didn't know or practice the principles of life affirmations nor did I recognize opportunities that were placed before me. You see, I didn't yet know my value.

Consequently, I played around when I was in high school. I was complacent about my grades; I didn't apply myself, and I really didn't know how to get what I wanted out of life. Again, God has ways of showing up and revealing your value. I can tell you had I not had family who urged me to join the military, I would have been married fresh out of high school and probably never left home. I was also blessed to have an uncle serving in the Air Force who encouraged me to join that branch of Armed Forces. This made it easy to set my sights on serving my country all while making money and going to college.

I was an introvert most of my life; however, now as an adult, I know that was due to my insecurities and my upbringing. I've learned along the way that it doesn't matter what value others place on you, it's the value you place on yourself. Your personal values will dictate what you think and how you behave. You are more than enough! Now do the work.

Keep a positive attitude. I recall a conversation with my four-star general as to the importance of aptitude versus attitude. She said that she would select candidates who possessed positive attitudes first (happy to do) over those with outstanding aptitudes (able to do). Her advice to me was that her prerequisite for a good team member were those persons who reflect positivity; as they are trainable, and most likely to enhance her team's ability to perform and to bring cohesiveness to the team at large. This, as opposed to someone who has the best skillset but whose negative demeanor and outlook could prove caustic to the team environment and have a negative impact on the success of the team.

This conversation helped me to understand the importance and value of attitude in our personal lives, as well as our workplace. I determined that it was important for me to have a positive attitude, to hone my skills and become the best I could be no matter what I was called upon to do or where I was placed. Just as having a positive attitude requires having gratitude, being grateful for what you have also allows you to reflect that positivity in all areas of your life and receive and attract more of what you're grateful for. If you are mindful to be grateful for your job; if you are grateful for your family; if you are grateful for others and grateful for God waking you up (because He didn't have to), it's impossible to be a "Negative Nancy" or a "Debbie Downer." Choose to be positive!

Hard work (not luck) pays off. I cannot discount hard work. I am willing to delay pleasure while pursuing my goal. Sometimes, it means I might have to study a little longer after my family goes to bed or get up early before they rise, even when I would rather sleep in. This allows me to be present with my family. Hard work for me means that I must constantly work at improving myself in order to bring value to others, even if it means delaying the vacation I had planned. Don't misunderstand me, I do take time for the things that bring me joy!

Because I also have learned to work smarter and not harder.

I have learned that some things I must do; but other things I have to be willing to entrust to others who have shown me or that I believe are adept at what they do! Their success makes me successful, too. There are times when I struggle to let go and let others do their job, but there are only 24 hours in a day. I can't be everywhere, and I can't be everyone to everybody. Therefore, having clear priorities and values helps me to quickly adjust my single-handed attitude and allow my fellow teammates to pitch in to accomplish the mission.

What about luck? I have to admit—sometimes, it *is* about being in the right place at the right time. This is called *opportunity*. However, you can be in the right place at the right time, and unprepared when opportunity comes a knocking, and you can get left out! I once heard the late Jim Rohn say, when opportunity meets preparation, that equals success" and that statement has stuck with me ever since. I work really hard at being prepared for opportunities. Now, I don't always wait for opportunities to come knocking. Many times, I create my own opportunities by not being afraid to take on a challenge. Remember, nothing beats *hard work,* not talent or even "luck."

Think About Your Vision

Write your vision down. You need to have a vision; make it plain and write it down. Remember to revisit and revise as often as you need to. After writing the vision, thank God for everything He has done and for what He is going to do. Then, let it go. Have faith that He will direct your path. *Thy word is a lamp unto my feet and a light unto my path* (Psalm 119:105 KJV).

I am a visionary by nature; therefore, I am more apt to plan for and pursue what I can see. Thus, once I have imagined it, I do well to write it down, and post it where I can view it as often as necessary. The reminders help me to not only track my goals, but to stay on track. With my business, I wrote my goals down (i.e., business plan), thanked the Lord for the vision He had given me and what He was going to do, and then I occupied myself with the hard work that opening a business required of me.

I was amazed when I looked back over my original goals, because I actually achieved the majority of the goals I had set for my business. I met several of the milestones set for my business within the first two years of the business. I am constantly reminded that, "I can do all things through Christ who strengthens me" (Philippians 4:13)! The same happened with setting goals with my family. We set goals to travel to places we had never been: Italy, England, Hawaii, etc. Those, too, came to fruition. As goals were met or achieved, I set new goals (and wrote them down). If they were not met, I addressed any issues or circumstances that prevented me from achieving those goals. In some instances, it required major adjustments to the process; and in others, only minor adjustments were needed. Still other goals were delayed or replaced with new ones. The point is, it is necessary that you start with a vision and write it down. Understand where you want to go, so that when you get there, you will know it.

My letter to Lil Lisa reminded her of God's value of her, her need to make mistakes and *learn* from them in order to become wiser (successful); how to love (value) others as she loves (values) herself; to put her best foot forward in all that she does; to take advantage of opportunity by being prepared; and to remind herself that life is a gift from God, so enjoy her journey! This is my advice to you as well.

Now go and give it your all and do all to the glory of God.

Signed,

Big Lisa

I know that life is truly a journey. I don't know at what point I realized it but, as my purpose manifested, this became clearer to me. Just as babies learn to roll over (stage of awareness), crawl, stand, walk (various stage of practice), then run (stage of mastery), life follows a similar pattern. I discovered my path through the many mistakes that I have both made and been spared (awareness). Along this journey, I have learned if it—whatever "it" is—works, then apply it. But, if it doesn't work, change course, (practice) and once you have perfected your gift, help others to help discover theirs (mastery).

Meet the Authors

Karen Bankston, PhD, MSN, FACHE, FAAN

Professor, Adjunct
College of Nursing at the University of Cincinnati
President/CEO
KDB and Associates Consulting Service LLC

An Adjunct Professor in nursing, Karen Bankston, Ph.D., M.S.N., FACHE, is the former Executive Director of the Child Poverty Collaborative, Cincinnati. A collective impact organization designed to lead the community's planning and implementation of efforts to ameliorate poverty by providing guidance on public policy, employment, housing, transportation, education and health care concerns. Previously she held the role of Associate Dean for Clinical Practice, Partnership and Community Engagement of the College of Nursing at the University of Cincinnati. In that role, she was responsible for developing and maintaining partnerships with nursing and other disciplines, while engaging in community-based research focused on student and parental success in the urban core. Additionally, she is the president and CEO of KDB and Associates Consulting Service, a company she founded after completing 5 years as the senior vice president/CEO of Drake Center, Inc., part of UC Health. Dr. Bankston previously served as the senior vice president of external affairs for the Health Alliance responsible for local, state and federal government relations, community relations, marketing and public relations. She also served as the external affairs liaison to neighborhood councils, the Uptown Consortium, United Way and other community agencies, and oversaw the Health Alliance departments of community health and diversity.

Prior to that she held positions as vice president of operations/chief operating officer and vice president for patient care/chief nursing officer at University Hospital in Cincinnati. She served as associate dean of clinical services and clinical assistant professor at the University of Cincinnati College of Nursing and Health. She also held nursing and nurse manager positions at Western Reserve Care System in Youngstown, Ohio.

She is currently a member of the boards of the Legal Aid Society of Greater Southwest Ohio, the LiveWell Collaborative and The Children's Home. In the past she served on the boards of the United Way of Greater of Cincinnati, the Urban League of Southwest Ohio, the Society of St. DePaul, the YWCA of Greater Cincinnati, to name a few.

She has been involved in the Cincinnati USA Regional Chamber's Agenda 360, Diverse by Design Committee, having served as its chair. She played a role in getting legislation changed for distribution of medication for the charitable pharmacy established by St. Vincent DePaul, and was a member of its founding board. She is founding chair and former member of the board of the Center for Closing the Health Gap and was responsible for the formation of this organization.

 She has received numerous awards and honors, including: 2017 Cincinnati Woman of the Year; American Nurses' Association Mary Eliza Mahoney Award 2016, University of Cincinnati Distinguished Alumni Award 2016, Kent State University Professional Achievement Alumni Award 2016, UC Kautz Leadership Alumni Award 2013, United Way James A. Hall Diversity Leadership Award 2010, University of Cincinnati Linda Bates Parker Legacy Award 2010, 2007 Corporate Woman of the Year–USA Regional Cincinnati Chamber of Commerce; 2001 YWCA Career Woman of Achievement Award; Business Courier Health Care Hero; Cincinnati Human Relations Pope Leadership Award; Girl Scouts Woman of Distinction Award, and Cincinnati YMCA Black Achiever. She is a member of Sigma Theta Tau, Delta XI, International Nursing Honor Society, the Queen City (OH) Chapter of the Links, Inc. and the Cincinnati Alumnae Chapter of Delta Sigma Theta. She is a graduate of Leadership Cincinnati Class XXVII.

Dr. Bankston earned an Associate in Applied Science (AAS) degree from Youngstown State University, a Bachelor of Science in Nursing (BSN) and Master of Science in Nursing (MSN) from Kent State University, and a doctoral degree (PhD) from the University of Cincinnati with a focus on administration and organizational behavior.

Updated Sept. 2018

Tywauna Wilson MBA, MLS(ASCP)CM

Booking inquiry: info@trendyelitellc.com
Website: www.coachteewilson.com
LinkedIn: https://www.linkedin.com/in/tywauna-wilson-55574630
Facebook, Twitter, Instagram: @coachteewilson
Leadership Training: www.trendyelitellc.com

Tywauna Wilson is a best-selling author, entrepreneur, and an award-winning leadership maven helping movers and shakers shift to the next level. She is the Owner/Chief Leadership Consultant of Trendy Elite Coaching and Consulting Services which she founded in 2017. Trendy Elite focuses on transformational change by equipping leaders with the tools and expertise needed to be successful influencers who inspire personal growth and leadership in the workplace and in their local communities. Trendy Elite offers a variety of training programs, leadership assessments, and coaching programs. In addition to the leadership training programs with Trendy Elite, Tywauna hosts a weekly international radio program called *Leadership Tidbits with Coach Tee Wilson* on Direct Impact Broadcasting radio and tv network in which she co-owns with her husband.

Tywauna started her leadership journey in the clinical laboratory as a medical laboratory scientist providing complex testing to aid clinicians in accurate diagnosis and patient care. Over the past 15 years, she served in a variety of progressive leadership roles, with her most recent being the System Technical Director of Chemistry for one of the top regional labs in the Dayton, Ohio community. In this role she provides clinical expertise, strategy, and collaboration to seven hospital locations and a core reference laboratory.

In 2018, Mrs. Wilson, co-authored her first best-selling publication, *"Dear Fear, Volume 2: 18 Powerful Lessons on Living Your Best Life On The Other Side Of Fear"*. This book challenges readers to push through fear and begin living the life they deserve. It gives them the strategies and tools they need to answer their questions of self-doubt and create a plan of action to move beyond their fear and into their greatness. Since then she has co-authored the following best sellers; *"It Takes Money Honey: Guaranteed Strategies to Wealth Creation, Proven Tips for Financial Freedom and Developing Faith"* (2019), *"Girl, Get Up and Win"* (2019), and *"Gyrlfriend Code: Sorority Edition (2019)"*.

Mrs. Wilson holds a bachelor's degree in Clinical Laboratory Sciences from Kentucky State University and a MBA from Indiana Wesleyan University. She has received several accolades including: 2019 Ambition Magazine List, 2018 Werking Women Award, 2017 American Society for Clinical Pathology Forty Under 40 Award, 2015 UC/UC Health Martin Luther King Jr Award, 2012 Girls Scouts of Western Ohio Leaders of Promise Award, 2011 Cincinnati Business Courier Forty Under 40 Award, and 2010 YWCA Rising Star Award.

Tywauna is actively involved in The Dayton Public Schools Foundation Board, Urban League of Greater Southwestern Ohio, John Maxwell Team (Executive Director), American Society for Clinical Pathology, Dayton BizWomen Insiders Club, and Delta Sigma Theta Sorority, Inc.

Tywauna enjoys traveling and creating new memories with her husband Martinez and their children Racquel, Martinez Jr, Caleb, and Brooke. When Tywauna is not spending time with family and friends, she enjoys reading and exercising.

Tashawna Thomas Otabil

God First| Family | Servant Leader| Mentor| Small Business Consultant | Motivational Speaker| Visionary | Results Driven Professional |Co Author

Tashawna Thomas Otabil currently serves as the Director of Managed Care for TriHealth a $2B Health System in Cincinnati, Ohio. She has nearly 20 years of Management experience and proven performance leadership with Managed Care Payer Contracting and Strategies. Tashawna is responsible for contractual relationship management valued at over $1.3 billion dollars in revenue.

Before joining TriHealth in 2017, she worked for both payer and provider organizations in various Healthcare leadership and administration roles. Tashawna received a bachelor's degree in HEALTHCARE Business Administration from DeVry University and she is a graduate of the Urban League of Greater Southwest Ohio Southwest Ohio, African-American Leadership Development Program.

She is passionate about achieving personal & professional growth. In January of 2019 she launched her own consulting firm. Tashawna Otabil consulting, a company geared towards developing innovate strategies for small businesses, professional or personal growth. She is also the Co-Owner and CFO for THOMAS Rehabbing, general contracting and Construction management.

Lastly, she's a speaker and co-author of "It Takes Money Honey" a book 365 day devotional about freedom faith and finances and working on her second book titled "Hidden Pain" a personal story of resiliency.

Tashawna is committed to public service and is actively involved in the community as a member of the Board of Directors for the Urban League of Greater Southwest Ohio, Southwest Ohio Healthcare Financial Management Association & the St. Aloysius organization. She has received several awards and recognitions for her leadership and service, including 2018 Top 15 Business Women of the Year.

Tashawna is the proud parents of two children (Malachi and Jordan). She enjoys cooking, traveling, leading and organizing community events. She spends her free time volunteering with youth ministries, mentoring small business owners, and developing young professionals.

Dr. Christine Handy

Chandy18@hotmail.com

Facebook – Christine Handy
Instagram- Christine_C_Handy

In her career span, Dr. Christine Handy has always been in a helping or coaching role. With more than 30 years as teacher, coach and high school principal, while an entrepreneur and author, Christine's life mission is to enhance the life of others via education, counseling, coaching, and partnerships.

A three-time Amazon best selling author, Christine has participated in three successful collaborations. Her chapter in *Dear Fear* shares memories about her arrival to college after being homeless during her senior year in high school. She challenges others to be like David, fearlessly fighting giants, and remember that David was victorious. In *It Takes Money Honey – Freedom, Faith, and Finances* and *The Purposed Woman 365 Day Devotional*, she shares inspirational and motivational words of wisdom and advice to live by.

Christine has enjoyed an amazing career in the field of education. She was recognized as the 2006 Maryland Secondary School Principal of the Year and was the 2014 recipient of the prestigious Dr. Edward Shirley Award for Excellence in School Leadership. She has spoken at numerous conferences across the USA and internationally in China. A respected leader in education, she presently serves as the President of the National Association of Secondary School Principals, the first woman of color to serve in this position.

Christine is also a proud entrepreneur, focused on helping others to be a member of the Comma Club (earning a check with a comma in it, month after month) and understanding the valued concept of residual income. A leader in the field, she strives to "change lives" via an entrepreneurial journey. She is also a trainer, coach, and speaker with the John Maxwell Group, specializing in presentations on "Leadership Matters" and leading teams through The Leadership Game. She loves helping others develop their leadership skills, grow their business, and to realize their financial dreams.

Christine serves as an usher at the Church of the Redeemer and is a proud member of Delta Sigma Theta Sorority, Inc.

Dr. Sharon H. Porter, (Dr. Sharon), is an Educator, Best-Selling Author, Publisher, and Interview Host. She has served as an educator for over 25 years as a classroom teacher, Test Development Specialist, Regional Instructional Specialist, assistant principal, Leadership Development Coach, and elementary and middle school principal.

She is a graduate of Winston-Salem State University, National-Louis University, The Johns Hopkins University, Walden University, and Howard University.

Dr. Sharon is the host of The I Am Dr. Sharon Show, a LIVE weekly in-studio interview show, owner of SHP Enterprise Inc. which consist of Perfect Time SHP LLC, Coaching, Consulting, and Book Publishing Firm, The GRIND Entrepreneur Network, Write the Book Now, and SHP Media. She is the Executive Director of the Next In Line to Lead Aspiring Principal Leadership Academy

She is a proud member of Delta Sigma Theta Sorority, Incorporated, International Association of Women (IAW), an Official Member of the Forbes Coaches Council, Sister 4 Sisters Network, Inc., and Professional Women of Winston-Salem.

Dr. Essie McKoy

Educator/Speaker/Author/Coach/Entrepreneur!

Dr. McKoy received her Doctorate in Education (Ed.D.) and an Educational Specialist Degree (Ed. S.) in Educational Leadership from the University of North Carolina at Greensboro, a Master's Degree in Middle Grades Education from Appalachian State University, and a Bachelor of Science Degree in Special Education with certification in Learning Disabilities from Winston-Salem State University. She has additional areas of certification in Public School Administration/Principalship, Curriculum and Instruction with a concentration in English, and the Superintendency. Her dissertation topic, "A Study of Elementary Principals' Perceptions of Accountability and Leadership in an Era of High Stakes Testing," is a foundational part of her book, "The Heart of School Transformation: My Journey into Transforming Urban Schools." She attended The Urban Superintendent's Program at Howard University and The American Association of School Administrators and received the National Superintendent's Certification. In addition, she attended Harvard University's Public Education Leadership Project Program and many other leadership programs throughout the nation, including the Wake Forest University Leadership Program for Public Engagement, The Distinguished Leadership Program and the Distinguished Leadership Program Digital Learning at North Carolina State University, The Principals' Executive Program – Leadership Program for Assistant Principals at the University of North Carolina at Chapel Hill and received the Program's Outstanding Academic Achievement Award and she graduated from the Principals' Executive Program – Leadership Program for New Principals at the University of North Carolina at Chapel Hill where she received the prestigious Jack McCall Award. Dr. McKoy also attended the Mastering Leadership Dynamics Program with the BB&T Institute, as well as three other programs at BB&T. In addition, she was accepted into The National Scholars Honor Society. A highlight of her career is that in 2017, she was selected by Winston Salem State

University as the Education Alumni Achiever Recipient.

Dr. McKoy began her teaching career at an alternative middle school and later taught at another middle school. She has served as assistant principal at the elementary level before becoming the principal of two elementary schools. She worked as an instructor at the Math and Science Academy of Excellence at Winston-Salem State University and worked as an Adjunct Professor at NC A&T State University and ITT Technical Institute. Furthermore, she served as an Executive Director/Principal. Her experience spans from pre-K through college and she use her experience and knowledge to continue to make an impact in the field of education! Dr. McKoy was nominated for the AASA Women in School Leadership Award with the Bill and Melinda Gates Foundation. In addition, she received the Educator of the Year Award and The Executive Citation of Anne Arundel County Maryland Award. Dr. McKoy has been featured in K.I.S.H., BSM, SwagHer, and UP WORDS (Edutopia) magazines. She has received many accolades and recognitions for her accomplishments throughout the span of her career.

She is known as a transformational leader and has improved the academic performance and success indicators of all the schools she has led. She is most proud of the fact that both elementary schools became Piedmont Triad Signature Schools! Her mission is to continue to ignite a passion in others and to make a profound impact in the field of education to help at-promise students believe and change the trajectory of their futures!

She started her own Educational Consulting Business, Dr. Essie Speaks, travels the nation to do speaking engagements, and published her first book about school transformation in 2018. Currently, she is writing more books and completed three co-authoring book collaboration projects thus far. They are: Coaching Champions- How to understand the players before giving the plays; A Guide to Improvement and Success, Women of Virtue: Walking in Excellence, and The Grylfriend Code Sorority Edition. In addition, she is the Senior Executive Director of the DMV Mastermind Organization and serves as a faculty member at George Mason University! Furthermore, you will see Dr. McKoy once a month co-hosting about educational topics with Dr. Sharon Porter on the, "I Am Dr. Sharon Show." The segment is entitled, "Education First."

She invites you to visit her web site at www.dressiespeaks.com.

Alandes Powell

Fifth Third Bank
Vice President, Business Controls

Alandes Powell recently joined Fifth Third Bank in October 2018 responsible for Controls supporting the various Lines of Business in Operations.

Alandes formerly served as Senior Vice-President and Director at Citi Cards, a division of Citigroup. She was responsible for the strategic development and oversight of a Portfolio within Cards Retail Services.

Mrs. Powell joined Citi in 1990 and has over 30 years of experience in the financial services arena. She also served as Director of Collection's Program Management Group where she directed initiatives supporting 13 sites and eight lines of business impacting over 3.5 million customers. She has held a number of positions at Citi including; Unit Manager, Trainer and Sr. Project Manager.

She is an active member of the community serving in a number of capacities over the years to include: Urban League of Southwestern Ohio Board of Directors, Past Chair of the Urban League of Greater Cincinnati Advisory Board, YWCA Board of Directors, Brighton Center Board of Directors, Assistant Director of a youth sports organization, Elder Board of Inspirational Baptist Church, Motivational Speaker for Adults and High School students and Prior Co-Chair of the Academic Scholarship Committee at Triumph Church. She is a graduate of Leadership Northern Kentucky, Urban Leadership Program, and member-alumna of Leadership Cincinnati Class 41.

Alandes currently serves as Board Chair of the Greater Southwestern Ohio Urban League and was the recipient of the YWCA Career Woman of Achievement in 2013 and Cincinnati Enquirer/Greater Cincinnati Foundation Woman of the Year in 2018.

A native of Dayton, Ohio, Mrs. Powell attended Fort Valley University an HBCU located in Fort Valley, GA. Alandes and her husband, Gordon are the proud parents of three children; 35 year-old daughter; Kendra (Atlanta, GA), 30 year old son; Damonte (Cincinnati Fireman) and 19 year old son; Julian (Clark Atlanta University).

Jaresha Moore, MBA

Founder/CEO of Empower On Purpose, LLC

Jaresha Moore, MBA is the Founder/CEO of Empower On Purpose, LLC , where we provide leadership training and personal and professional development coaching and consulting services; Certified Coach, Speaker and Trainer for the John Maxwell Team, best-selling author, success and empowerment coach with over 18 years of combined experience in Education, Finance, Healthcare, and Business Management and Development; Owner of Envisioned Broadcasting Radio Station and host of Empower Hour with Jaresha.

Born and raised in Dayton Ohio, Jaresha 's passion lies in motivating, inspiring and empowering emerging leaders, entrepreneurs, and business professionals who are developing their leadership skills and businesses. As a single mother of 4, Jaresha identifies with the challenges that one faces with adversity, fears, self-doubt and the many obstacles that life tends to send our way. As a result, she has used her experiences and training to build a successful brand, business and legacy for her children. Jaresha believes that when life gives us lemons, that is a way to not only make lemonade but turn it in to an opportunity to use that lemon to teach and empower others.

As a John Maxwell Certified Coach, Teacher, Trainer and Speaker, Jaresha offer's workshops, seminars, keynote speaking, one-one-coaching, group coaching, mastermind training, and e-courses, aiding the personal and professional growth of her clients through study and practical application of proven leadership methods.

Jaresha is a member of (WiBN) Women in Business Network, (NAPW) National Association of Professional Women, (ACHE) American College of Healthcare Executives and (POWER) Professional Organization of Women of Excellence Recognized and an active Board Member of Human Race Theatre Company.

Email: admin@empoweronpurpose.com

Facebook: www.facebook.com/empoweronpurpose

Instagram: www.instragram.com/jareshamoore

Website: https://www.empoweronpurpose.com

Maya N. Dorsey

My name is Maya Dorsey. My resume includes fourteen years of diverse educational experiences. After spending some time in education, I earned a second Master's in Educational Leadership with an Ohio Principal Licensure from Antioch University Midwest in 2015. I wanted to broaden my literacy knowledge so I earned a Reading Endorsement from Wright State University in 2014. I earned my first Master's in Elementary Education from Grand Canyon University in 2008. In 2004 I earned a earned a Bachelor's of Science Degree in Organizational Leadership and a Minor in Women's Studies from Wright State University.

My years of experience includes roles as a teacher, literacy coach and school administrator. I have worked in urban school settings most of my career. My goal has always been to be a positive example to students and their families who look like me and have shared similar experiences as me.

In my current role I serve as a Director of Family Engagement and Community Partnership with Learn to Earn Dayton. I oversee a cohort of out of school time professionals who participate in a Summer and Afterschool Collaborative that was birthed out of Mayor Nan Whaley's City of Learners initiative. Additionally, I support local school districts within Montgomery County on initiatives related to third grade reading, eighth grade math, culturally responsive teaching, and equity coaching. My work gives me the opportunity to work with community professionals who are passionate about changing the landscape of education in Dayton, OH.

Community service work is close to my heart. Five years ago I felt compelled to start a non-profit organization aimed at mentoring school aged girls. From that idea The Girl's Project Inc was developed. Our mission is to prepare, inspire and empower girls to be their best version of themselves.

The Girl's Project's metrics include:
- Academic focus grade level completion and high school graduation
- Good school attendance
- Exposure to career and college readiness skills & STEAM
- Community Service Projects
- Emphasis on exposure to literature

Highlights/Core Competencies:
- Founder and CEO of The Girl's Project Inc. www.thegirlsproject.us
- Partner with Girls Who Code
- Partner with Fastforward Sinclair Community College
- Partner with Mentoring Collaborative Sinclair Community College
- Member of Dayton Chapter of the LINKS incorporated 2018
- 2016 Educator of the Year Award Rotary Club, Above and Beyond Award Recipient, and Who's Who Among Teachers Recipient 2007
- Co-Founder of Dorsey Den Podcast
- Co-Author of Leadership Tidbits Leadership Book
- Human Capital Management
- Organizational Development

Professional Development:
- Learn to Earn Dayton Readiness Summit Planning Committee member
- Culturally Responsive Teaching workshop Training by Zaretta Hammond
- Participated in Oak Park River Forest series screening on STARZ network
- Trauma 101 Trainer
- Equity Fellows Coach
- Featured Speaker on Think TV Social Emotional Learning Filming National Summer Learning Association (NSLA) conference
- Bias Habit & Breaking training with DPS & Preschool Promise
- Equity Training from National Equity Project
- Educational Leadership Coach

- Ohio Afterschool Network (OAN) conference
- COSEBOC conference
- Racial Equity Workshop
- National Family Engagement Conference
- Strive Together Conference

Natalie Ocean Canty

An energetic, strategic, and thoughtful business professional, Natalie Ocean Canty has spent her career as an administrator, business developer, and project manager. For the past 13 years, she has worked at universities focused on nontraditional student recruiting, developing partnerships, and advancing institutional branding. She creates develops multi-level contracts with corporations, government agencies, and community colleges. Her gifting area is administration, which she applies to each project. She enjoys mentoring and sharing what she likes to call "life nuggets" with others. She uses her platform to foster positive personal brand development and career advancement.

Natalie is a native New York from Brooklyn and currently resides in Cincinnati, OH with her husband. She is a graduate of the New York City Public School System and matriculated at the City University of New York (CUNY)-Borough of Manhattan Community College. She earned a bachelors degree in business management, masters of business administration (MBA), and post-graduate certificate in project management from University of Phoenix.

August 2019.

Crystal Cooper. Ed.D

Leadership-Culturally Responsive Teaching-
Social Emotional Learning

Booking Inquiry: drcrystalcooper2018@gmail.com
Instagram: @PrincipalCooper
Facebook: Principal Cooper
LinkedIn: https://www.linkedin.com/in/crystal-cooper-ed-d-912a2319
Twitter: @drcooper74

Dr. Crystal Cooper is a best-selling author, national consultant teacher, presenter, speaker, and an award-winning school principal,coaching other leaders in and out of the educational industry in various facets of leadership, culturally responsive teaching, literacy and social emotional learning research and implementation.

She is the developer of Principal Cooper®, Professional Learning Consulting Services, LLC, which she is presently in the midst of launching this year. This PC-PLCS focuses on supporting schools and businesses across the nation with pathways to improve school and work environments and processes that build positive work spaces for children and adults. PC-PLCS offers a variety of professional learning workshops, and coaching opportunities focused on many areas in education and business.

Dr. Cooper earned a doctoral degree in Educational Leadership from the University of Georgia, a Specialist degree from the University of West Georgia, a Masters degree from the University of Georgia and a Bachelor's degree from William Paterson University.   During her undergraduate years, she was highly involved, serving as the president and a member of several clubs, treasurer of the student government, resident assistant and homecoming queen.

Crystal began her leadership journey in the classroom where she taught grades 1-4 for seven years in Paterson, New Jersey. Over the past 16 years, she served as a literacy coach, assistant principal, national presenter/consultant with her most recent being the school principal of award-winning Title I school in a large district outside of Atlanta, Georgia. She is a nationally certified consultant teacher for the Center for Responsive Schools®, graduate of the Learning Forward Academy, and Gwinnett County Public Schools' Quality-Plus Leadership Academy.

In her recent role as principal, she provides instructional expertise, culture building and instructional coaching for a large faculty of over 100 staff members and 850 students. She supports and coaches her staff in building high-quality and engaging lessons that infuse social-emotional learning and culturally responsive teaching tenets into the everyday curriculum. She is known as an expert in leading and providing a positive work environment that is engaging, memorable and meaningful.

In 2019, Dr. Cooper, co-authored her first best-selling publication, Power of Kingdom Mindset . This book is an anthology of believers who share personal testimonies around various principles. She is presently collaborating on a book titled Leadership Tidbits (December 2019). A collection of leadership strategies and tips from leadership trailblazers in different industries who share practical ideas centered on help to develop others in the area of leadership, personal growth & development, mindset, or communication.

She has received several accolades including: Teacher of the Year, Herald News Golden Apple Teacher of the Year, and for mentoring others to greatness in their careers. As principal, she has earned recognition for superb teaching and learning, while helping children achieve at high levels academically, socially and behaviorally.

Crystal is actively involved in the Lanier Education Foundation Board, National Coalition of 100 Black Women, Hands on Atlanta, and Delta Sigma Theta Sorority, Inc. She serves as a volunteer and leader on a charter school board, and at her church. She continues to desire to leave a legacy in helping others feel empowered and capable of conquering their dreams and goals. She also enjoys traveling and creating new memories with her family and friends. When Crystal is not spending time with family and friends, she enjoys reading and exercising.

Crystal's greatest strengths are her drive, positive mindset and leadership qualities. Her most recently recorded strengths according to the Strengthsfinder® assessment are: Communicator, Woo, Input, Connectedness and Positivity. Additionally, she was assessed in the past as a learner, achiever and as responsible. She shares these

results with others, to give them insight into her philosophy on leadership and also how her participants can become stronger leaders, when they know their own strengths.

Known as passionate, fun-loving and loyal, Crystal is excited to continue expanding her journey as a published author and creator of a new educational consulting business that will work to cultivate positive educational experiences for children, teachers and leaders across the world in all areas.

Dr. Melissa Brunson

A skillful and accomplished educational leader and advocate of 23 years, Dr. Melissa Brunson serves as the special education supervisor in the Montgomery County Public Schools (MCPS) Department of Special Education Services and previously as the principal of Cloverly Elementary School for nearly 12 years. In addition to this role, she has served as the "voice" for elementary school principals as the vice president of the elementary chapter and board member of the Montgomery County Association of Administrators and Principals.

In addition to working full-time as an educational leader in MCPS, she serves as an adjunct professor at Howard County Community College in Howard County, Maryland. She earned her Bachelor of Arts in Sociology at Montclair State University, which is located in New Jersey, and a Master of Arts in Leadership in Teaching at Notre Dame University, which is located in Maryland. In 2015, she received her Doctorate in Educational Leadership from Bowie State University, which is also located in Maryland. Her many affiliations include being a member of Phi Delta Kappa, Sigma Gamma Rho Sorority Inc., Chi Alpha Honor Society, Golden Key Honor Society, and the National Association for the Advancement of Colored People. She is also an active member of Life Change AME church, where she serves as a co-leader of the Couples' Ministry, Circle of Faith Women's Ministry, and former educational administrator of Kidz Zone, the Children's Ministry.

As an extension of her doctoral work, Dr. Brunson has helped to lay the groundwork for elementary principals within her district to receive ongoing technology leadership professional development. She is personally passionate about ensuring that every child has access to technologies in order to advance their digital literacy skills. Additionally, she has taken steps to empower potential teacher leaders to serve as mentors and/or consider leadership positions where their skills could be best utilized. In her role as principal developer, she's supported and built the instructional leadership capacity of aspiring administrators, assistant principals on the track to become principals, and a principal intern, who have all progressed to becoming instructional leaders in their respective schools. She led roundtable and panel discussions at educational conferences and meetings, including but not limited to the International Conference on Urban Education, Young Education DC Professionals, and the American Enterprise Institute, focused on principal leadership in the 21st century.

Dr. Brunson genuinely affirms the belief that all students deserve excellent leaders and teaching staff and must be educated in healthy and hopeful school environments where their academic potential is maximized. She is inspired by the borrowed quote, "You can be the reason some student gets up and comes to school when his life is tough. You can be the reason some student 'keeps on keeping on' even though her parents are telling her that she can't succeed. You can inspire your at-risk students. Remember that as long as you are a teacher, even on your worst day on the job, you are still some student's best hope." (Educational Leadership 2002/January 2003, Strategies that Close the Gap, p. 34). In her everyday walk, she aspires to be a part of the reason why more and more students, particularly those who are affected by poverty and other intersecting challenges, are acquiring the skills to be college and career ready.

Dr. Arthur Williams

Dr. Arthur Williams is the youngest of nine children to the late Squire and Joyce Williams. Arthur grew up in the "North Philly"section of Philadelphia. Arthur graduated from Benjamin Franklin High School in 1989. After high school, Arthur attended Millersville University in Lancaster County, PA. He earned his Bachelor's of Science Degree in Education in 1993. After a short return to Philadelphia after college, Arthur served as a substitute teacher in the Philadelphia Public School System. In 1994, Arthur accepted a full time social studies teaching position with the Dorchester County Public School System located in Dorchester County, Maryland. While working in Dorchester, Arthur completed his Master's of Arts Degree in School Administration from Salisbury State University in 1999. Arthur continued his teaching career by joining the Montgomery County Public School System in 1999. Arthur has served as a teacher, assistant principal and principal. Presently, Arthur serves as the "Proud Principal," in Silver Spring, Maryland. In 2013, Arthur successfully defended his dissertation and earned his Doctorate in Leadership and Policy Studies from The University of Maryland at College Park. His dissertation topic was, *"Teacher Leaders' Perception of Distributed Leadership Practices in Middle Schools.*

Arthur is an affiliate instructor with Hood College and Loyola University Graduate School of Education. Arthur also served as a member of the Interagency Collaboration Board (ICB) of Montgomery County, Maryland from 2014-2016. Arthur serves on the executive board of the Maryland State Association of Secondary Principals.

Arthur is the proud father of two energetic boys - Caleb (7) and Asher (5). He is the husband to his lovely wife, Carla Fisher Williams who serves as a professional school counselor.

Lisa Coker

Principal and CEO, Infinite Management Solutions

Lisa Coker is the CEO of Infinite Management Solutions, LLC, a woman veteran-owned certified, small business which primarily partners with middle-market and large organizations in both private and public sectors. Coker is a proud United States Air Force veteran. Throughout her career she has earned a reputation as a trusted partner, dynamic facilitator, outstanding problem-solver, and accomplished professional. A major accomplishment involved her leading a 120-member team in a strategic planning project for the Air Force Materiel Command (AFMC) 4-Star General Commander who oversees a $60 billion budget and over 80,000 employees.

As a certified Lean Six Sigma Black Belt practitioner, Coker partners with C-Suite executives to develop their strategic plans and streamline operational processes resulting in reduced operational costs and improved mission effectiveness. Coker has a bachelor's degree in Business Administration and master's degree in Organizational Change Management. She holds memberships to, Armed Forces Communications & Electronics Association (AFCEA); Women in Business Network (WIBN); Women in Defense (WID); and Rotary Club of Dayton. The Dayton Business Journal recognized Coker as one of the region's brightest young professionals and named her a 2018 "Forty Under 40" award winner. Coker continues to strive for excellence and gives back to her community. She was named to The American Business Journal's 2018 national list of Influential Young Executives, Rising Stars. Rising stars spotlights 100 people in business across the country who are having an impact relatively early in their careers on their companies and their communities.

In her spare time, Coker enjoys running, reading, and traveling with her husband and three children.

Thank You!

Thank you for reading Leadership Tidbits "Powerful Strategies Every Leader Needs to Know in Order to Win".

If you were able to learn and grow from this book, please take a moment to write a review as your words truly make a difference. Reviews can be made on Amazon.com or you can send us an e-mail at Leadershiptidbitsbook@trendyelitellc.com with the subject line "Review".

If you are interested in sharing your nuggets of wisdom as a coauthor in Leadership Tidbits 2, please visit us at www.leadershiptidbits.com or send us an e-mail with the subject line "Coauthor" at leadershiptidbitsbook@trendyelitellc.com.

If you are interested in leadership training and coaching, please visit www.trendyelitellc.com.

www.ingramcontent.com/pod-product-compliance
Lightning Source LLC
Chambersburg PA
CBHW061519050726
47593CB00002B/639